Unless Recalled Earlier

Date Due

JUN 1 6 1987			
OCT 1 9 1988			
APR 1 4 1989			
DEC - 1 1989			
FEB - 5 1991			
MAR 1 0 1993			
MAR 1 8 1994			
MAY 2 5 1995			
MAR 2 1 19__			

HANDLING GRIEVANCES
A Guide for Management and Labor

HANDLING GRIEVANCES
A Guide for
Management and Labor

Maurice S. Trotta

The Bureau of National Affairs, Inc.
Washington, D.C. 20037
1976

HD
6490
.G7
T76

Library of Congress Cataloging in Publication Data

Trotta, Maurice S
    Handling grievances.

    Includes index.
    1. Grievance procedures.   I.   Title.
HD6490.G7T76   658.31'55   76-42311
ISBN 0-87179-237-0

Printed in the United States of America

To Walter W. Bishop
and also to my wife, Margaret,
who has an unusual understanding of human nature.
As a result she successfully supervised
forty employees over many years.

Preface

Given the nature of human beings and the diverse objectives of management and labor, grievances in the workplace are inevitable. The arbitration process has become the method universally adopted by both management and labor in the public as well as private sectors to resolve those grievances that cannot be amicably settled by the parties.

However, if management and labor representatives involved in the grievance-arbitration process in both sectors understood the causes of grievances and followed some well-established principles on how to avoid them, or to settle them when they arose, the amount of time, money, and aggravation spent handling them could be substantially reduced.

The object of this book is to convey to representatives of both management and labor a working knowledge of how each can contribute to the reduction of grievances or their prompt settlement without the need of a formal arbitration hearing. Illustrations of situations that lead to grievances will be drawn from actual cases that have been submitted to arbitration.

Good labor relations depend in large measure upon the relationship between the shop steward and the foreman or supervisor, because this is where grievances usually start. Higher union officials and management representatives, who also become involved in the settlement and arbitration process, can contribute to better labor relations.

If this book succeeds in making it possible for all those involved, in both private and public sectors, to reduce the incidence of grievances and increase the number of grievances amicably settled without the need of final and binding arbitration, the author will consider his time and effort well spent.

I want to acknowledge here the contribution of Walter W. Bishop, an old friend and collaborator. His long years of experience as an industrial relations executive have provided many of the examples of actual grievance situations described in this book.

I also want to express my appreciation to Shirley Shields, who has typed the manuscript, for her exceptionally good work.

Sparta, N.J.   MAURICE S. TROTTA
March 1976

Contents

1 | General Causes of Grievances

[handwritten marginalia: ALTHOUGH TOPIC ARISE, NOT GOALS TO INABLE UNIONS TO SETTLE]

When we speak about labor-management relations, we are talking about the interaction between the employee, his union representatives, and representatives of management. We are dealing with human beings in a work situation. These human beings, whether they represent management or labor, have certain basic characteristics in common which must be understood if we are to succeed in avoiding grievances in the first place, or in settling them when they arise.

[handwritten marginalia: IN OTHER WORDS IF THEN PROB., COMM., IN RIGHT WAY]

COMMON HUMAN CHARACTERISTICS

Self-Interest

The most outstanding characteristic of human nature is self-interest. As applied to the work situation, it means that an individual, irrespective of his role, will evaluate each situation in terms of how it will affect him.

If management institutes a new work procedure, it will be viewed as good or bad by the individual employee in terms of his income, opportunity for overtime, working conditions, and so forth.

Management, on the other hand, will evaluate new procedures in terms of increased productivity and lower costs. In general, each will think of his own needs and give little attention to the needs of others. Conflict resulting in grievances is the inevitable result. Each side will then find reasons to support his position and oppose the other side with righteous indignation.

1

The Authority Complex

In modern society some individuals have authority to direct the activities of others. In a family, parents exercise authority over their children. The proper way to exercise this authority is currently the subject of much discussion.

In elementary and high schools, teachers and principals traditionally have authority over students. This, too, is the subject of controversy. Does this authority extend to the manner of dress and hair styles of students?

In modern business and industry it is essential that some people (management) plan and supervise the work of others (employees). Management cannot fulfill its economic function of producing goods and services unless it has the power to plan its economic activities and direct the work force. This involves making decisions which directly affect employees, and it is the exercise of this essential decision-making power by management which gives rise to many grievances.

Even within labor unions, shop stewards, people on the grievance committee, and other union officials have the authority to make decisions which affect union members.

When management makes a decision regarding the application of a provision of the contract and the union decides that management's interpretation is incorrect, a grievance results.

Grievances are also generated when the individual employee, or his union representative, objects to the manner in which management exercises its authority. Determining whether the employee is justified in his objections depends upon the behavior patterns of both the individual and his foreman or supervisor.

Some employees object to any type of authority. This may be a carryover from childhood when they resented an overbearing and dominating parent. People's reactions to those who exercise authority vary widely. At one extreme there are individuals who resent all supervision. At the other are people who, like the old European peasants, accept autocratic behavior on the part of supervisors as the normal way of life. One hundred years ago laws relating to employee-employer relations were called the laws of master and servant, a reflection of management's view of its authority at that time.

Today modern management concepts emphasize managers' responsibility rather than their authority. Democratic procedures are supplanting autocratic attitudes. In fact, the whole concept of the employee's right to file a grievance, found in all union contracts and even followed by some non-union companies, is a manifestation of this new trend which questions the absolute authority of management. Today it is accepted that employees should not be subject to arbitrary and capricious decisions, that no employee shall be disciplined except for "just cause," and that an impartial third person called an arbitrator has the power to make a final and binding decision.

To point up the authority complex as a common cause of grievances, let us review some actual cases heard by the author.

• An employee with many years of service was given a two-week disciplinary suspension because he talked back to his foreman in a loud and aggressive tone of voice. The arbitrator was asked to set aside four consecutive days for the hearing because the nine employees in the department wanted to testify on behalf of the suspended employee. At the hearing it developed that this department had worked without a supervisor for many years, until management promoted an employee from another department to be the new supervisor. He was given no supervisory training before his assignment to his new job. Moreover, management admitted that on occasion he exercised his new authority with a heavy hand.

The testimony revealed that even a good, experienced supervisor would have had some difficulty because the men in the department were not used to being supervised and resented supervision per se. It was also clear that the supervisor was impressed with his new authority and got satisfaction from ordering people around. He had also developed an authoritarian tone of voice.

Important Points

1. Authority must be used properly, even tactfully, to be truly effective.

2. Management should have personally explained at a department meeting why the assignment of a supervisor was necessary.

3. Management should have made sure that the man selected was well qualified and that his personality would enable him to gain the nine men's respect and confidence.

4. He should have been given whatever training he needed to handle his employee relations problems well.

5. A radical change from no supervision for several years could be expected to cause resentment and suspicion, especially because the nine men would consider the supervisor an "outsider" in that he was not one of their own department.

6. The desire of all nine men to testify in behalf of the grievant was prompted by their need to express their resentment directly to management.

• In another case the supervisor was a former Marine captain who gave orders in a crisp, impersonal tone. He was an efficient manager but was resented by his subordinates. One day he ordered one of his long-haired subordinates to operate a particular production line. It was obvious at the arbitration hearing that the employee chose not to hear the order and was suspended for insubordination.

Important Point

This supervisor failed to recognize that orders must be given differently in industry than commands to Marines. Workers invariably resent orders given in a manner which implies, "Obey me immediately because I'm your BOSS."

Workers feel they deserve to be treated as intelligent people. They want to know why the order is given as well as what it means.

• Another case involved an employee who was a member of the union negotiating committee and a shop steward. He was given a disciplinary suspension for using abusive language to his foreman, and filed a grievance. During the arbitration hearing it came out that during contract negotiations he had used foul language but, because he was on the negotiating team, it was tolerated. It was obvious that this shop steward was impressed with his own importance and new authority and took a delight in talking in an arrogant and abusive way to management.

• In still another case a union member with 10 years seniority was disciplined for insubordination and filed a grievance. After a week of hearings it was clear that he felt that his union membership enabled him to defy management with impunity.

Important Points

1. The two cases above illustrate how newly acquired authority can exalt a person's feeling of self-importance.
2. Although foul language may be tolerated during heated, controversial contract negotiations, such language should be avoided as much as possible by both union and management representatives.
3. Membership in the union and long service with the company do not absolve anyone from obeying instructions and established rules.
4. Shop stewards and other union members who acquire power sometimes abuse it.

After hearing cases for over 30 years, the author has come to the conclusion that most people do not know how to exercise authority, and that in order to reduce grievances, both union and management representatives must be given intensive training in this area. In the absence of such training, employees who are promoted to management frequently assume that to act like a supervisor one must be somewhat autocratic. This may be the result of working under autocratic supervisors. Some college graduates who are assigned managerial responsibilities think and act as if the people they supervise who do not have college degrees are inferior human beings. They do not even extend them the courtesy of listening to their complaints.

Union shop stewards and other union officials, if not properly trained, often delight in showing off their new-found power, particularly in dealing with management representatives. This is the cause of many arbitration cases, and may be the result of long years of resentment toward management, in some cases justified but oftentimes not.

• In one situation a regional director for the United Mine Workers disrupted an arbitration hearing by constantly interrupting the attorney for the company while he was presenting his case. He stopped when the arbitrator threatened to resign. Subsequently he apologized privately to the arbitrator, explaining that he had been a member of the union since the age of 10 when he had begun working in a coal mine in West Virginia, and that if the union had not been aggressive and belligerent, working conditions and wages would never have improved. He found that the only way to get results was by aggressive fighting, and it was difficult for him to accept a judicious approach to the solution of labor-management disputes.

Communications Barrier

Many grievances are caused by the failure of human beings to communicate properly. People communicate with each other by means of the spoken and written word as well as by what is colloquially known as "body language." Good communication takes place only when the concept in the speaker's or writer's (sender's) mind creates the same concept in the listener's or reader's (receiver's) mind.

Important Point

If the receiver doesn't get the intended concept, the sender hasn't communicated. The sender is responsible for ensuring that the receiver understands his message completely.

A problem arises when a spoken or written word has one meaning to the sender and a different meaning to the receiver.

• A supervisor of hospital records received a call from a physician requesting Mrs. Jones' medical records. He went to one of his employees and said: "Mrs. Jones' medical records are needed by Dr. Smith right away." The young lady immediately took out the records and placed them in the outgoing box, where a messenger picked up the contents every 30 minutes. About 15 minutes later Dr. Smith called angrily and said he was waiting for the records. The supervisor blamed the employee for not delivering them personally, and the employee resented the reprimand. She felt that if the supervisor had wanted her to hand-deliver the records, he should have said so. Obviously a climate was created that might well lead to a grievance when another incident occurs.

Important Points

1. "Right away" did not mean the same thing to the employee as to the supervisor. The order to her should have been more specific.

2. Meanings of words may be different depending upon the education and cultural backgrounds of the persons involved.

• In another example the issue before the arbitrator was the interpretation of a contract stating: "In making shift assignments seniority will be taken into consideration." An employee on the night shift requested a transfer to the day shift and was refused. He filed a grievance on the grounds that another employee with less seniority was selected to work on the day shift.

The evidence revealed that the union had made a demand during negotiations for seniority to be the sole criteria in shift assignments, and that the company had refused on the grounds that many other factors had to be considered for efficient production. It was finally agreed that the company would consider seniority as one of the factors.

From the evidence it was clear that the president of the union, in explaining the new contract, had merely told the members of the union that seniority was written into the contract, conveying the idea that it was the sole factor. Obviously he did not accurately communicate the agreement reached.

Important Point

All pertinent information must be fully and accurately communicated to employees by their officers.

• In another case a supervisor told the plant manager that he had assigned Mr. Doe to work in a different department because one of the men in that department was home ill, but that Mr. Doe had refused to do the work and gone home. The manager called Mr. Doe at home and summarily discharged him, and Doe filed a grievance. When the manager was cross-examined, he admitted that Mr. Doe had told him that he told his supervisor he felt sick and unable to do the heavy work assigned to him and was, therefore, going home. The manager testified that he thought Mr. Doe had made up the story about being ill to excuse his refusal to work, because the supervisor had not told him that Mr. Doe claimed to be ill. At the end of several hours of testimony it was clear that Mr. Doe had an excellent work and attendance record and had, in fact, told his supervisor that he was too ill to do the heavy work assigned to him, but that this information had not been communicated to the manager. This grievance was the result of poor communication and the failure of the manager to investigate before making a decision.

Important Points

1. Statements are sometimes distorted in favor of the sender, either purposely or unconsciously.

2. It is necessary to check the information by questioning the grievant or impartial persons and checking records.

What is communicated is also determined by the sender's tone of voice, facial expressions, and body movements, such as hand movements, shoulder shrugs, and so forth. Words spoken in an angry, aggressive tone will convey a different meaning than the same words spoken in a normal, conversational tone.

Important Point

Tone of voice, facial expression, gestures, and other body language are as important as spoken words, and sometimes even more so, since they give insight into the sender's attitude, which might alter the meaning of the spoken words and thus convey a different message.

Self-justification

Most human beings resent having their decisions questioned and will find innumerable reasons why their decisions are right. It is not difficult for a person to find reasons, satisfactory to himself, to justify what he has decided, even though his justification may be based on unverified assumptions and opinions. In the case of Mr. Doe, discussed above, the manager justified his summary discharge by the false assumption that the employee was not telling the truth.

    • In another case a foreman on the night shift spent about an hour on and off looking for one of his men, whom he finally found during the man's "lunch break" at 3:10 a.m., sleeping in the foreman's office. He asked another foreman to observe him asleep. They both waited until 3:32 a.m., two minutes after the lunch break ended, and then the foreman summarily discharged the employee for sleeping on the job. A grievance was filed. During the course of the hearing it developed that the employee was never given the opportunity to explain that he had not been able to be found because the man he was assigned to work with had asked him to go to another building to get something. If the foreman had given the employee the opportunity to explain, the story could have been verified.

The foreman justified the summary discharge by saying the man must have been asleep the entire time. In addition, he argued that the man should not have been asleep during his lunch break.

The tendency to justify what you have done even when wrong is a characteristic common to all people, be they union officials, foremen, managers, or deans of colleges.

Important Point

Everyone tends to try to justify his decisions, whether or not the rationale is correct.

Gut Reactions

• While conducting a conference on grievance handling at a military air base, the author described a typical work situation which had been the subject of a grievance, and asked one of the conferees, a highly educated electronics expert, how he would have decided the issue if he had been the arbitrator. The conferee gave his decision promptly, and when asked why he had made that particular decision, replied: "It was a 'gut reaction.' " When questioned further he said he did not really know why he had had that gut reaction. After discussing the case, it was evident that many of the man's fellow officers did not agree with his decision, which came as a big surprise to him because he was convinced that since he had wanted his decision to be objective and fair, it was in fact, and he thought everyone would agree with him.

The discussion which followed was most illuminating. It clearly demonstrated that the decisions even well-educated people make are the result of a lifetime of experiences, culture patterns, economic status, role playing, assumptions, opinions, and so forth, and that in most cases the decision maker is not even aware of why he feels and acts the way he does and how his feelings enter into his decisions. A shop steward whose father or grandfather was an old-time union leader who lived and worked under bad conditions and constantly expressed his dislike for the "bosses" will be conditioned to react one way, whereas a manager brought up in a family that looked down upon workers and damned unions as the cause of all economic troubles will be conditioned to react differently. Yet seldom does either person know why he reacts the way he does; he just feels he is right and thinks up arguments to justify his position.

Important Point

"Gut reactions" may be misleading because they are opinions and attitudes which result from the individual's conditioning by his lifetime experiences, and may not be objective.

• At the conclusion of an eight-week training session one foreman told the conference leader that his wife wanted to thank him for the course. The leader, surprised, asked what the foreman's wife had had to do with the training conference. The foreman explained that during one of the sessions a considerable amount of time had been spent discussing the need for foremen to develop the art of listening with the intent of understanding what the speaker was trying to communicate. When he went home that night, he realized for the first time in his life that he constantly interrupted people and made decisions without really understanding what they were trying to communicate, and this included his wife and children. He said that since he had stopped doing this his family life had been much better.

Important Points

1. The foreman had not been aware of what he was doing. Most people are surprised when their personality defects, which often generate conflict in the plant and at home, are pointed out to them.

2. Listening with sincere desire to understand the speaker's message is essential. The speaker should not be interrupted, and the listener should try to look directly at him or her.

Summary

In order to handle grievances effectively, it is important to understand how the average human being interacts in a work situation. Most people, whether employees, union representatives, or management representatives, will exhibit common characteristics, which bear restating.

1. Self-interest, or the law of survival

People are egocentric, and each person will look at a situation in terms of how it will affect him personally. A shop steward may file a grievance if he thinks his political aspirations within the union will be advanced if he is aggressive toward the company. A foreman will often fight a grievance because he thinks it might lead to a promotion.

2. The authority complex

Being able to give orders to other people generally inflates one's sense of importance. However, employees generally resent following orders given in an arrogant manner. It is interesting to note, however, that these same employees often become arrogant themselves once they are promoted to a supervisory level.

3. The communications barrier

Spoken and written words are often misunderstood. What is communicated is determined as well by the tone of voice, fa-

cial expressions, and other body movements—"body language"—of the sender.

4. Self-justification

Once a decision is made, the decision maker will most often
try to justify it, even when he knows he has made a mistake.

5. Gut reactions

Most people react to situations in a particular predetermined
manner, without knowing why. Moreover, they assume that
their reactions are correct and that most other people would
react in the same way.

COMPANY CLIMATE

By company climate we mean the character of interpersonal
relationships that permeates the entire company. Whether
there is a high or low incidence of grievances is often determined by the climate in which people work.

Top Management Attitudes

The attitudes of top management usually filter down to lower
level supervisors. If top management people, in their dealings
with management and nonmanagement employees, listen to
and exhibit consideration for other people's ideas and gripes,
give credit where credit is due, and otherwise establish good
personnel policies and practices, others in the organization
will tend to behave in a like manner. Unfortunately, contrary
attitudes exhibited by top management will also be followed
by subordinates.

People who are anxious to move up in an organization
will tend to acquire the characteristics of those who have the
power to promote them. This is a very pragmatic approach because, in general, the managerial ability of persons being considered for promotion is measured in terms of how closely
their managerial style conforms to the style of those making
the decisions. It is normal for most people in top management

positions to think that their own managerial style is the best. Their proof is the fact that they now hold the position they do. They give little thought to whether they arrived at this top position because they purposely followed the previous top manager's style, or happened to have the same style to begin with, were related, or belonged to the same social set as the person giving the promotion.

During the past 25 years, graduate schools of business have conducted much research into what constitutes a good manager. Put simply, a good manager is one who can effectively utilize the human, mechanical, and material resources under his direction to turn out a product or a service at a reasonable price and make a fair profit.

In recent years we have come to realize that the manager's most difficult function is the effective utilization of human resources and that his greatest asset is his ability to work with and through people. The growth of unions has emphasized the importance of this asset.

The grievance-arbitration process, which has become an essential component of almost all collective bargaining agreements, has made managerial decisions subject to analysis by an arbitrator who has the power to modify or revoke them. While the textbook image of a top executive as a person who never makes a decision except upon all the facts, has no thought of personal gain, uses only objective analytical methods, and always makes fair and objective personnel decisions is not universally applicable to all executives, it is no longer possible for managerial decisions affecting union members to be arbitrary and capricious, or based upon unverified assumptions and allegations or personal biases. The assumption made by most people that if a man is discharged there must be something wrong with him is now highly questionable.

In recent years much evidence has been disclosed to show that some executives, even those at the highest levels of government whose decisions vitally affect issues of war and peace, boom and depression, inflation, unemployment, and so forth, can make serious errors in judgment.

A new breed of executive is emerging, however, operating on a higher ethical level and making sounder, more objective decisions. These people are helping to create the type of company climate which reduces internal tensions, creates more job satisfaction, and reduces the incidence of grievances.

Important Points

1. Company climate, although sometimes rather intangible and difficult to define, is an important element in providing job satisfaction and pleasant working conditions. It has a marked effect on the incidence of grievances.

2. Top management sets the basic tone which permeates the company, but the union and the manner in which grievances are processed also influence company climate.

One person who worked for a medium-sized brokerage firm on Wall Street stated that he would not change his job even if he were offered $2,000 more a year in salary. When asked why, he responded that everyone liked to work for this company because top management was not only considerate and fair, but was sincerely concerned about the welfare of each employee.

A former student who worked for IBM was promoted to a managerial post. Before he assumed his duties he was required to take a one-week course in the elements of good management. The first sentence spoken by his instructor, one of the company's top executives, was that his first objective as a manager is to be sure that the people under his supervision are happy. His second is to meet production standards. However, if he succeeded in meeting the first objective, he said, his second would usually take care of itself.

• A union official in Puerto Rico expressed the view that it would be impossible to unionize a particular plant of 3,000 employees because the employees felt that top management was sincerely interested in their welfare.

• In a different company, I was engaged to conduct a series of training conferences for managers, supervisors, and foremen. In preparation, I interviewed all the managers, and was told in confidence by one manager, who had been with the company for 20 years, that none of the managers knew where they stood, and that he, for one, would not be surprised if he were fired with 24 hours notice. This was a clear indication of a company climate which discouraged loyalty to the company. I thought, however, that he was exaggerating until the following incidents occurred: The personnel manager, who had been with the company for many years, arranged on Thursday to meet me on Saturday morning to discuss some matters connected with the training program. On Saturday the son of the owner met me instead. When I asked if the personnel manager was ill, he told me that he had been given his discharge notice the night before. The son was now personnel manager, even though his qualifications were nil (he had been a fighter pilot during World War II). Moreover, he stated that he would attend all the training sessions and pick out the "dead wood" foremen and fire them immediately.

When I told this young man in the open meeting that he could not judge a foreman's ability by how he spoke at a training session, and that no decisions should be made without first consulting the managers, it was like exploding a small bomb. Thereafter all the managers expressed to me in confidence their dissatisfaction with the climate in which they had to work, and all began to look for new jobs.

Important Points

1. Employees prefer to work for a company which has a good company climate, and where management is considerate of them as individuals. Consequently, they do a better job.

2. A bad company climate may cause employees and supervisors to be fearful about the threat of losing their jobs.

• The author was selected to arbitrate 35 grievances for one company, some of which were 18 months old. (There were 75 additional grievances still pending, for which arbitrators had not yet been selected.) After the first three days of hearings, it was evident that labor-management relations were characterized by such mutual distrust and antagonistic attitudes that none of the grievances had ever been intelligently discussed. Each side was merely out to win.

Several years later a very highly qualified new industrial relations head was appointed, but he resigned after one year. When asked why, he said that he could not work effectively in the antagonistic climate he felt was generated by top management, and that he could not do an effective job with untrained personnel in his department.

Important Points

1. Mutual distrust and antagonism between management and the union cause a bad company climate, which obstructs the resolving of grievances.

2. It is essential that people in personnel administration be well qualified.

During arbitration proceedings it frequently becomes obvious that a bad company climate has prevented intelligent discussion and amicable settlement of problems. Although top management usually determines company climate, sometimes no matter what management does to create a good climate, the union is so unreasonable and antagonistic that the company cannot succeed in creating a good climate.

• About 400 grievances were filed by a union representing the employees of a very large manufacturer. The author was one of many arbitrators selected to hear these grievances. At the first hearing, even though a court reporter was present, the president of the union, who was very belligerent, placed on the table a tape recorder, saying he wanted to take a recording of the hearing and play it back at the next union hearing to show the rank and file what "s.o.b.s" the company officials were. The company objected to the presence of the tape recorder, and the arbitrator upheld the company's objections. The union walked out of the hearing, objecting strenuously to the ruling. About a month later it was learned that an entirely new team had been assigned to handle the company's industrial relations, and new union officials were elected. Thereafter, almost all the 400 cases were settled.

Personnel Policies

It is not possible to have a good company climate without good personnel policies. There are many good text books on personnel administration that describe what constitutes good personnel policies.

The following is a listing of some *bad* personnel policies and practices that inevitably lead to grievances:

1. Jobs not classified according to job requirements;
2. Employees doing the same work but receiving different wages;
3. Employees assumed to be wrong, with no investigation of supervisor's allegations.
4. Inconsistent application of personnel rules and union contract;
5. Favoritism;
6. Bad working conditions.

Employee Selection Process

If the selection process is haphazard and the employee is over-qualified or underqualified for the job, grievances will result.

• A personnel manager in Puerto Rico explained that previously he had always selected the person with the highest I.Q. test score to fill all positions. An analysis of turnover indicated that in certain departments turnover was very high and many grievances arose. These departments had most of the routine, dead-end jobs, which did not require a high I.Q.

Thereafter the manager selected people with a lower I.Q. to fill these positions, and turnover rates and grievances declined in those departments.

Important Point

An employee whose I.Q. is appreciably higher than required by the job will soon become dissatisfied and bored because the work is not challenging.

Supervisor Selection Process

If top management selects foremen only on their mechanical know how and their ability to keep the union in its place, they are inviting trouble. The ability to supervise people effectively is of critical importance. A first-class machinist is not necessarily a first-class supervisor.

Training Policies

Many people in management circles now realize that the amount of training needed to make a good supervisor is appreciable. Unless a company makes a conscious effort to give its foremen and managers the skills needed to perform their supervisory duties, the efforts of top management to create a good climate and reduce grievances will fail. Moreover, it is unfair to promote a person to a supervisory or managerial post without training and then criticize him for not doing his job properly.

The shift from a nonsupervisory to a supervisory job involves a complete change in attitude and responsibilities. Most people cannot make this change without help in acquiring the new skills needed.

Important Points

1. The skills and other qualifications necessary for a supervisor differ considerably from those for the employees supervised.

2. Ability to direct the work of others is one of the supervisor's most important qualities, an ability not required by a good worker.

3. Newly appointed supervisors usually need training in supervisory skills.

UNION ATTITUDES

Some union officials do not know how to handle labor-management problems. They assume a belligerent attitude toward management which precludes intelligent dialogue and problem-solving.

Attitude of International Representatives

The attitude of a union's international representative can either foster good labor-management relations or aggravate labor problems. Many are intelligent men who perform their duties in a nonexcitable, businesslike manner, who have sometimes expressed the view that they have more trouble with belligerent and frequently unreasonable local union officials than with management. They often have to "cool down" excitable local representatives.

However, some international representatives are themselves belligerent and unreasonable, and these attitudes permeate the thinking of rank-and-file members as well as local union officials.

International representatives usually play an important role in drawing up demands and negotiating contracts. They may lead local representatives to believe they can succeed in obtaining certain high wage and pension settlements, and thus create conditions that may lead to a strike. If, during negotiations, they become abusive in their language, or make generalized statements to management such as "You made a lot of money this year," or "You are overworking your employees," without knowing the facts, they are helping to create a climate that will lead to grievances and strikes.

● During one arbitration case the international representative who presented the case was belligerent, and constantly interrupted other people, and spoke abusively to management representatives. On the second day a different international representative continued the case, who had an entirely different attitude. He spoke little, but what he said was pertinent to the issue. He never interrupted the proceedings, and addressed management in a positive, courteous manner. The American Arbitration Association's representative explained the reason for the change as follows: The international representative at the first hearing had until recently handled most of the arbitration cases, but had been replaced by the second man whom, however, some last minute emergency had prevented from appearing on the first day. He explained that the union discovered the nonbelligerent man won more cases than the aggressive one.

Important Points

1. Union leaders are responsible for the union's climate in the same way that management is for company climate. Bad union climate can cause strikes and grievances.

2. International union leaders should avoid giving local leaders the impression that they can gain excessive wages and benefits for them.

3. International leaders should also set a good example for the local union in negotiations with the company by avoiding generalizations and by a nonabusive approach. A calm, factual, nonabusive approach usually wins more for the union than unreasonable, belligerent demands.

Attitude of Local Union Officials

If top local union officials take the attitude that they are out to "get" management, this will influence the thinking of shop stewards and rank-and-file members. As a result, more grievances will be filed, and fewer will be settled without arbitration. Another result of this attitude is that they will probably also fail to get all the facts, and will advance emotional, not logical, arguments. Consequently, they will lose many arbitration cases.

The attitude of shop stewards is often a critical element in determining how many grievances are filed and how many will be settled.

When shop stewards are elected by the rank and file, there is a possibility, particularly when the company climate is antagonistic to the union, that the person elected will be the most belligerent and vociferous one, because he is expected to express to management the feelings of the employees.

When shop stewards are not properly trained to perform their duties, and remain belligerent and vociferous, the number of grievances is sure to rise and the chances of settlement are slim indeed.

Summary

Although some grievances are the result of honest differences of opinion, many are the result of the failure of human beings to understand how to get along with each other. This is complicated by the fact that representatives of labor and management, because of different objectives, evaluate problems differently and develop attitudes that aggravate grievances and hinder settlements.

2 | Specific Causes of Grievances

The immediate cause of a grievance may come from the employee, the supervisor, or the shop steward. In this chapter, an analysis will be made of how the behavior patterns of each can cause grievances. If we can recognize the types of behavior that cause grievances and eliminate them, we will have taken a long step toward reducing the incidence of grievances.

THE EMPLOYEE AS A SOURCE OF GRIEVANCES

Very frequently the employee himself is the cause of grievances. Management often has good reasons for disciplining certain employees. The purpose of this section is to point out those employee characteristics which frequently lead to grievances.

It is interesting to note that the employee himself is often not aware of his own shortcomings and will try to justify his actions. As a result, when management decides to discipline him, he will file a grievance claiming that the action taken by the company was not justified.

Qualifications Do Not Match Job Requirements

An employee's mental and physical abilities must match the job requirements fairly well or the employee may become a problem employee. If a person's ability and skill are appreciably above the level required by the job, he or she will get no satisfaction from doing the work, will become bored, and is unlikely to perform well. Unless such an employee is promoted or transferred to a more challenging job, he or she will probably eventually find something to complain about, or will resign.

• This is exactly what happened in the personnel department of a large company. This company used intelligence and aptitude tests as an aid in selecting new employees. Two clerks spent all their time scoring these tests, a routine job which required only average intelligence, but did require a high degree of clerical aptitude and complete accuracy. When one of the clerks resigned, the employment manager was unable to find another woman who had just the right qualifications. He finally hired a woman with excellent clerical aptitude but somewhat higher than average intelligence. The new woman did an excellent job for the first two or three months, then gradually began to neglect her work, spent an excessive amount of time away from her desk, made an occasional careless error, and even interfered with the other clerk's work by talking to her too much.

When her boss, the employment manager, reprimanded her for her errors and for interfering with the other clerk's work, she said she wanted to resign because she didn't like the job. He was not surprised, knowing that she had the ability and intelligence to perform more challenging work. He told her there would be an opening for an accounting clerk in about one month, and that he had in mind recommending her for this job. She was pleased with this opportunity, went back to her job, and did good work again until she was transferred to the accounting department. The more challenging job gave her sufficient job satisfaction, and she was content to remain with it for several years, until she received another promotion.

When a person's ability and skill are below the level required by the job, a different but possibly more troublesome problem will develop. When the employee finds he cannot do the work properly, he feels frustrated and usually becomes antagonistic, and then will find something about which to grieve. If the supervisor reprimands him about his unsatisfactory work, he is likely to feel picked on, and eventually his resent-ment will result in a grievance. This certainly will happen if the employee is unaware of his shortcomings, as is frequently the case.

Important Point

An employee's overall capability, as indicated by mental capacity, temperament, and personality, should match the requirements of the job fairly well or the employee will probably become dissatisfied and be unable to per-form the work satisfactorily.

The only answer to the problem of an unqualified employ-ee may be to transfer him (or her) to another job for which he is qualified, or to terminate his employment. The supervisor should, however, try to determine the exact reason for the em-ployee's incompetence. It may be due to lack of sufficient edu-cation or aptitude for the kind of work involved. On the other hand, it may be due to insufficient on-the-job training, in-adequate instructions, misunderstandings, or some other cause over which the supervisor has control. The supervisor should question himself as to whether he has given the em-ployee adequate training, or whether his orders have been clearly understood. Unless his honest answer is yes, the super-visor should try again through additional training or by clari-fying his instructions and making sure that the employee com-prehends. This is not always easy, because the employee may be somewhat nervous, may lack the self-confidence that he can please the boss, and may be timid about asking questions which might make him appear stupid. Frequently an employ-ee will say he understands, rather than take the chance of hav-ing his supervisor consider him dumb.

Personal Problems of Employees

Even when an employee is well qualified for his job and has the proper degree of intelligence and aptitude, he may become a problem because of some outside influence. If a normally stable employee should become irritable or otherwise show a change in behavior, the supervisor should determine the cause before disciplining him. Frequently the employee will be unaware of the change. If ill health or a temporary family problem is responsible, patience and tolerance on the part of the supervisor may be the best approach. Employees are sometimes hesitant to reveal their personal problems for fear they may lose their jobs, especially if the problem is ill health. The supervisor should determine the reason for the change in the employee before imposing discipline, if at all possible.

• In one case an employee who had many years of service and a good work record was reprimanded by his supervisor because he was frequently late or absent. After repeated warnings and a one-week disciplinary layoff, the employee was warned that his next offense would result in a discharge. Upon his next absence he was discharged. He filed a grievance.

At the hearing it was disclosed that the employee had been embarrassed to tell management the reason for his poor attendance record. He finally revealed that his only son had come back from Viet Nam a drug addict and his wife had become emotionally disturbed because of this. He described in detail how his record of lateness and absence was directly caused by his efforts to help his son. After learning the facts, management offered to cooperate with the employee and rescinded the discharge.

Important Points

1. An employee's performance is sometimes adversely affected by influences not related to the work situation, such as emotional disturbances due to a family or health problem.

2. The supervisor should try to determine the cause of any change in an employee's behavior pattern.

Unreliable, Uncooperative, and Antagonistic Employees

A tactless, uncooperative, and unreliable employee who generally has a sour attitude is likely to become antagonistic to his supervisor when reprimanded. Such an employee probably grew up in an environment where tact, cooperation, and reliability were not considered virtues; it follows that he cannot understand why he is being disciplined by his boss. A reprimand or more severe discipline may aggravate the problem unless properly administered. The reason must be carefully and fully explained in terms he can comprehend and accept or the supervisor will probably have a formal grievance from him.

Important Points

1. Discipline must be carefully administered to recalcitrant employees whose cultural background and life style are different.
2. The supervisor must make sure that the employee fully comprehends the reasons for the discipline.

Linguistic, Racial, and Cultural Problems

If an employee cannot understand the language spoken by his supervisor and other employees in the shop, he may often become suspicious and misinterpret what has been said.

In one case, a Spanish-speaking employee who had been denied workman's compensation became convinced that his employer had prevented him from receiving compensation benefits. The union lawyer, who did not speak Spanish, could not convince him otherwise. His antagonism toward his employer eventually led to a grievance.

Many employees belonging to minority groups that have been discriminated against for many years are extremely sensitive and claim discrimination when none exists. If they are reprimanded for poor workmanship, lateness, or absenteeism, they immediately assume that they are being discriminated against and will file a grievance.

Persons brought up in one culture will develop behavior patterns different from those of people brought up in another way. In cities like New York, where a great variety of cultures exists, employees of one culture are often supervised by those of a different culture.

• An employee born in a small village in Egypt was employed by a hospital in the United States. He was discharged as being emotionally unbalanced and in need of psychiatric treatment due to the following incident: On one occasion he had felt ill, and went to the outpatient clinic for treatment. They did not think he was seriously ill and told him to go into an adjacent room and lie down. He was left alone for about two hours and became very upset because he did not receive any medical attention or medication. A loud, emotionally charged argument resulted. He explained that he had become upset because his mother had died in Egypt as the result of lack of medical attention. The hospital staff saw no logical reason for his emotional outburst and considered him emotionally unbalanced.

It is interesting to note that the employee involved felt that Americans were strange, unfeeling people because when he attended a funeral, nobody exhibited any emotion. In Egypt, as in some other countries, it is customary for persons to cry and show great emotion at funerals, whereas in our culture we are taught not to show our emotions. Such conflicts in culture are often the cause of grievances.

Union Membership

There are some employees who feel that because they are union members they are immune to disciplinary action. They acquire the attitude that the union, not management, is running the shop, and that if they do not like management's decisions they are free to ignore them or to call a strike. They even ignore grievance-arbitration procedures and insist on having their own way. If an employee is disciplined, he believes that the union will exert enough pressure on the company to reverse its decision. Obviously such an attitude on the part of the employee and union officials will be the cause of many serious grievances.

The function of a union is to negotiate a labor contract and be sure the company lives up to the provisions agreed upon therein. It is not the union's function to manage the company. If the union feels that the decisions made by the company violate the contract, it has the right to file a grievance, and an arbitrator will ultimately decide who is right.

THE SUPERVISOR AS A SOURCE OF GRIEVANCES

Unfortunately, some supervisors are responsible for causing grievances because of incorrect decisions or failure to take proper action when they should. Supervisors should subject themselves to honest self-examination from time to time to discover whether they are guilty of the kinds of action which can precipitate grievances.

Wrong Attitudes

A supervisor's attitude toward the union is often the cause of grievances. Particularly when a company has recently been unionized for the first time, supervisors and managers often resent having their decisions questioned and having to answer formal grievances. This is particularly true at military installations where civilian employees are unionized. The military men who manage these installations find it difficult to operate under a union contract and have shop stewards and other union officials question their decisions. In the military it is not customary for subordinates to question their superior's decisions. Therefore, when a person trained in the military acts as a manager of unionized civilian employees, he has a very difficult adjustment to make.

Under these conditions it is understandable when a military manager subconsciously resents the union and tends to ignore the contract. The U.S. Civil Service Commission has conducted many conferences designed to make military managers realize that the law permits unionization of civilian employees, and that whether they personally approve of it or not, union contracts must be adhered to and employees be recognized as having the right to file grievances and ultimately to have the issues decided by an arbitrator.

If a supervisor's attitude is antagonistic or arrogant, he is likely to act in a manner which will irritate his subordinates, thereby causing grievances. An arrogant supervisor usually issues orders in a heavy-handed manner and reprimands employees with little or no reason. A supervisor's attitude of "Do as you are told because I'm the boss" in issuing an order will be resented, particularly by an employee performing work which requires a relatively high level of knowledge or skill. He will resent being made to feel small; his personal dignity will be offended. Such arbitrary and inconsiderate action by a supervisor inevitably irritates employees and causes grievances.

A supervisor's antagonistic attitude can only cause resentment. The employee will probably be so angry he will not accept a reprimand even when deserved; hence it will, at best, be ineffective. At worst, it may be the spark which ignites a grievance.

Weak Supervision

The opposite of the tough, arrogant supervisor is the weak supervisor who fails to command proper respect from his subordinates. This type of supervisor also can cause grievances. Employees want their supervisor to be a self-confident leader who controls his department in all respects.

When a weak supervisor permits an employee to get away with something, the other employees lose respect for him. Certain strong-willed employees may even try to assume authority they should not have, and all employees are likely to become lackadaisical and try to get away with doing as little work as they can. Under these conditions friction, disagreements, and bickering develop among employees.

Unjust Discipline

Undeserved or excessively harsh discipline may cause grievances. Such unjust discipline is almost always due to the supervisor's failure to control his emotions, or his failure to get all the facts before imposing discipline. If a supervisor loses his temper and disciplines an employee while still angry, he is unlikely to be objective. He will probably impose a penalty more severe than is warranted by the employee's act. The supervisor should cool off, make sure he has all the facts concerning the incident, and then determine what discipline is justified. Unfair discipline is almost sure to cause grievances, and he may even find that the facts do not justify discipline of any kind.

Favoritism and Inconsistency

Favoritism shown by a supervisor is almost certain to cause grievances eventually. Inconsistency on the part of a supervisor is a form of favoritism. If he reprimands one employee for tardiness but overlooks the tardiness of another, permits one employee to leave early yet denies the same privilege to another, he is favoring certain employees and discriminating against others. This will cause grievances. A supervisor must treat all employees fairly and impartially; it is important not only to be consistent, but also to avoid any appearance of inconsistency.

Promises to Employees

Promises should seldom be made to employees, but any promise made by the supervisor should be fulfilled, or else the employee will have a grievance. Supervisors must be careful to avoid statements which can be interpreted as a promise. All of us are prone to read into other people's statements just what we want to hear, and sometimes an employee will regard a supervisor's casual remark as an implied promise. For example, if a supervisor tells an employee that he is considering him for transfer to a better job, the employee will probably think of this as a promise of promotion. If he is not promoted, he will feel that he has a justified grievance.

Failure to Eliminate Sources of Irritation

Failure to detect and eliminate conditions which irritate employees will cause grievances.

• A machine operator working on a piecework basis complained to his foreman that the trucker had not removed three pallets of castings which he had machined, and had not delivered additional castings for him to machine. The foreman agreed to have the pallets removed and additional castings trucked to the operator's machine, but failed to do so. About 20 minutes later, the machine operator located the foreman and again registered his complaint. The foreman replied that he had forgotten the original request because he had gotten involved in the emergency breakdown of another machine, and said he would take care of the problem right away. However he again failed to do so. Fifteen minutes later the operator went to the foreman and angrily demanded that the castings be moved immediately. Both men became angry. The operator cursed the foreman, and the foreman discharged him on the spot for abusive and profane language. This resulted in a grievance which was eventually settled by arbitration.

Obviously, a machine operator on a piecework basis will become irritated if a situation beyond his control causes him to lose money. The foreman in this case agreed that the operator's request was reasonable, but failed to take proper action. There would have been no grievance if the foreman had followed through and had the castings moved.

Sometimes the source of irritation is not as obvious as in the case described, but an alert supervisor who detects and removes sources of irritation promptly will save himself trouble, prevent grievances, and gain his employees' goodwill.

Important Point

A supervisor may be responsible for causing grievances by his actions or lack of action in many ways, particularly by failing to follow through on a promise made to an employee.

Unclear Orders and Inadequate Instructions

If an order is not clear or if the employee does not completely understand it, it may cause a grievance.

• A supervisor told a clerk, "Mr. Jones needs those records," intending to convey the idea that the clerk should deliver them in person immediately. The employee followed the usual practice of putting the records in the outgoing mail box addressed to Mr. Jones. Two hours later, after the records had been picked up but before they were delivered, Mr. Jones called the supervisor and angrily complained that he had not received them. The supervisor bawled out the clerk in public, then told her to find the mail boy and get the records to Mr. Jones in a hurry.

Important Points

1. The clerk had a justified complaint since she had followed the established procedure by putting the records in the interoffice mail box.

2. The supervisor was wrong in failing to tell her to deliver them in person to Mr. Jones immediately, and in publicly reprimanding her.

Inadequate instructions, like unclear orders, can also cause grievances. This applies particularly in the case of a newly hired employee. A new employee may be experienced in the type of work he is assigned, but the supervisor must assure himself that the employee knows exactly what he is supposed to do, how he is to perform the work, and the results expected. In addition, the supervisor should show him where to obtain special tools if required, materials and equipment needed, and should explain the procedures he should follow. If the new employee is inexperienced in the work he is to do, the supervisor should instruct him thoroughly.

Unless orders are clearly understood by employees, and unless employees are properly instructed, misunderstandings will occur and cause grievances. It is the supervisor's responsibility to ensure that his subordinates fully understand his orders, and that they are properly instructed to do their work.

Important Point

What the employee understands is more important than what he has been told.

Some supervisors are better trainers than others, but any supervisor whose ability to train employees is inadequate should concentrate on acquiring this skill. It will make the job as supervisor easier in the long run, and will help him to eliminate one cause of grievances.

Failure to Keep Employees Informed

Employees are entitled to know about any changes planned by management or by the supervisor which will affect them in any way. Any change planned should be communicated to them as soon as possible after a definite decision has been made to effect the change. It is not enough merely to announce the change; the reason for the change should be explained. The employees should be given an opportunity to ask questions and get answers.

People normally react negatively to changes at first. We are governed largely by habit. We learn to accept existing conditions, and we are suspicious or even fearful of any change to be imposed upon us. But if a proposed change is fully explained in advance, most people will give it a try, especially if the change can reasonably be expected to provide some kind of advantage.

Failure to Dispel Rumors

In addition to keeping employees fully informed about changes, a supervisor should take prompt action to dispel rumors, because rumors can cause grievances. Rumors crop up from time to time in all companies. Some turn out to be true, but most rumors are not based on facts or, at least, they exaggerate the true situation. A supervisor should be alert to detect rumors and dispel them by giving the employees the facts. Sometimes a rumor can be dispelled only by official statements from top management. In any case, rumors should be counteracted promptly to prevent loss of morale and avoid grievances.

Important Point

Supervisors should keep employees informed of any changes which may affect them in order to avoid false rumors.

Failure to Listen and Consider Employees' Viewpoints

Employees should be given the opportunity to express their viewpoints. In fact, supervisors should seek their viewpoints and suggestions.

A supervisor should not always assume that employees are wrong. He should get the employee's viewpoint and consider it before making a decision. The first step in considering the employee's viewpoint is to listen carefully and patiently to him. Beyond listening, the supervisor may have to search for what the employee is trying to convey to him, which may require questioning in order to understand the employee's viewpoint fully. He should not make any decision until he gets all the facts. Having obtained and completely understood the employee's point of view, the supervisor should evaluate it objectively, and should then tell the employee whether he agrees, agrees in part, or disagrees with him. If he does not fully agree with the employee's viewpoint, he should explain his reasons and try to change the employee's point of view by persuasion. If he agrees with the employee, he should tell him so and take proper action if action is called for. Failure to listen and consider the employee's viewpoint may cause a grievance.

Important Points

1. A supervisor should listen carefully to an employee to ensure that he understands the employee's viewpoint.
2. He should give the employee his decision only after carefully evaluating this information.

Failure to Consider Employees' Best Interests

If a supervisor acts in a manner which obstructs an employee's progress or otherwise affects an employee's best interests, a grievance may result.

• A typical example is the case of a supervisor who tried to prevent a young man from transferring to a better job in another department. The young man had worked as a stock clerk for three years after graduation from high school. During this time he attended night school at a nearby university, taking mathematics, accounting, and other courses in business administration. He had developed an interest in electronic data processing and had decided that he would like to become a computer programmer. When he learned that his company was planning to establish a new data processing department, he asked the warehouse foreman's permission to discuss a transfer with the man who had been selected to be the head of the data processing department. His foreman refused, telling him he could not be spared because he was the best stock clerk and the warehouse was extra busy.

A few weeks later several types of IBM machine were installed in a rearranged space in the company's office building. About the same time, the clerk saw the company's newspaper ads for IBM operators and operator trainees. He again approached his foreman, who again told him no. He decided then that he had a justified grievance, but as he left the foreman's office on his way to find his shop steward, he happened to meet the personnel director, who stopped to talk with him. The personnel director noticed that the young man was upset and asked him what was troubling him. The outcome of the incident was that the personnel director persuaded the foreman to let the clerk transfer as soon as he could hire a suitable replacement for the warehouse. Had it not been for the chance meeting of the personnel director and the clerk, the foreman would have been faced with a grievance, one he probably would have lost.

Important Point

No supervisor likes to lose a competent employee by transfer to another department, but when the transfer is beneficial to the company or is a deserved promotion for the employee, the supervisor should not try to block it.

His attitude should be that no employee, even though important to him, is irreplaceable. He can even be a bit proud that one of his employees has been selected for a promotion or for a transfer which will benefit the company. The supervisor who stands in an employee's way because of an "I can't do without him" attitude certainly will cause a grievance, or the employee may even resign.

Incomplete Understanding of Labor Contract

Supervisors in unionized companies must have full knowledge and complete understanding of all contract provisions which can possibly affect their operations. Failure to abide strictly by the contract provisions nearly always causes grievances; any violation of the labor agreement justifies a grievance, and the union will undoubtedly present one.

Supervisors must, of course, know their company's employee relations policies also, especially if they supervise any employees not covered by a union contract. A supervisor who fails to live up to a company policy which affects employees is likely to cause a grievance. If, for example, company policy gives senior employees certain privileges, such as choice of vacation period, the supervisor should abide by the policy unless he can get the senior employee to agree to give up the privilege. If the employee is unwilling to waive his right and the supervisor arbitrarily refuses to grant it, a grievance will probably be the result.

Not only should the supervisor know the contract, company policies and rules, he should make sure his subordinates understand them. Although each employee may have a copy of the union contract and an employees' handbook containing company policies and rules, there will be occasions when the supervisor will have to interpret them. He should welcome the opportunity to explain when an employee asks questions or does not fully understand, as this will avoid misunderstandings which could cause grievances.

Important Points

1. A supervisor must thoroughly understand the provisions of the labor contract and the company's personnel policies, and should make sure his subordinates understand them as well.

2. He should welcome questions as an opportunity to avoid misunderstandings which could cause grievances.

THE SHOP STEWARD AS A CAUSE OF GRIEVANCES

The shop steward plays an important role in the grievance-arbitration process. He is a critical factor in labor-management relations. What he says and does and how he handles situations will often determine whether a formal grievance will be filed. Many international unions conduct special training programs for shop stewards because they recognize the fact that a shop steward needs special skills to perform his duties. Merely because an employee is interested in union affairs does not qualify him to be an effective shop steward. Discussed below are some of the errors commonly made by shop stewards which cause grievances.

Incomplete Knowledge of Labor Contract

Unfortunately, some shop stewards do not have a working knowledge of the labor contract and only assume they know what it says and means. As a result, they may give employees who complain erroneous information.

• In one situation a senior employee on the night shift was refused a transfer to the day shift. He complained to his shop steward that a junior employee was given the transfer in violation of the seniority clause of the contract. The shop steward agreed with him and filed a grievance. The case was lost in arbitration because he did not read the contract carefully. The contract provided that seniority was only one of the factors to be considered in making a transfer, not the sole criterion.

Important Point

Shop stewards, like supervisors, must understand the labor contract thoroughly to avoid mistakes in processing grievances.

Making Unwarranted Promises to Members

A shop steward who makes a promise he cannot fulfill, or who gives an employee false hope by exaggerating what he can do for him, can cause a grievance. If an overly aggressive steward creates the impression that he can do almost anything for the union members he represents, he will be unable to convince an employee with an imaginary grievance that he does not have a valid grievance. If this occurs the steward may find himself in a position where he will have to process an unwarranted grievance.

Similarly, if a steward misinterprets the contract to an employee or gives the employee incorrect information for any reason, this may cause a grievance. In one case a steward caused a grievance by giving three employees incorrect information, because he had failed to get all the facts.

• A company had obtained permission from the city to use city-owned property directly in front of the main building for 12 parking places. The company paved this area, and reserved four spaces for the use of company executives and eight spaces for vendors and other visitors. A large parking lot for employees' use was just across the street. For more than two years the reserved spaces were used as intended by the company. On rare occasions when an employee attempted to park in one of these spaces, a company guard would point to the sign showing that these were reserved spaces and ask the employee to park in the employees' lot across the street. No employee had refused to do so.

The steward decided that, since the city owned the property where the reserved spaces were located, he and other employees had as much right to park there as anyone else. He convinced three employees to join him in parking their cars in the reserved spaces one morning. The guard asked the four men to move their cars across the street to the employees' parking lot, but they refused. The guard reported the incident. The outcome, after several unsuccessful attempts by the personnel director and other management officials to get them to move their cars from the reserved spaces, was that all four were given disciplinary suspension without pay. The steward and the three other men filed a grievance which eventually went to arbitration. The arbitrator decided that the company was justified, since the city had permitted them to use this space for reserved parking and employees had complied with the company's ruling regarding these spaces for more than two years. The steward should have investigated and discovered that the city had given the company permission to use city property for this purpose before he told the men to park there.

Important Points

1. A shop steward should avoid misleading an employee, such as by telling him he has a justified grievance when the steward is fully aware that the grievance is imaginary.
2. Stewards should carefully avoid misinterpreting the contract to employees.

Failure to Act on Union Members' Minor Complaints

If a union member makes a minor complaint to his steward, the steward should take proper action. This may be merely to give factual information to the employee, or to convince him that he does not have a valid complaint, or to convince the supervisor that he should take action to eliminate the problem. But whatever action is required should be taken. Neglect may cause the minor gripe to develop into a serious grievance. Employees' problems are important to them, and stewards should take them seriously and try to resolve them. They should never be brushed aside.

Showing Favoritism

Stewards, just as much as supervisors, should guard against favoritism. Stewards dislike certain people and like others, just as all people do. If a union member who is a close friend comes to his steward for assistance on a grievance or some other problem, the steward's natural reaction will be to go all out for his buddy. But the steward should follow the sound practice of getting the facts, evaluating them, and then deciding, as objectively as possible, what action he should take, just as he would if the individual were not his close friend. This is not easy to do, but it may be easier to be objective in such a case than when the situation is just the reverse.

A union member whom the steward dislikes deserves the same considerate treatment as a personal friend. The steward should not let his bias obstruct justice for an employee he dislikes. On the other hand, he may have to discount a loud-mouthed employee's complaint until he has made a thorough investigation. It is important, though, that the steward make such investigation regardless of his personal feelings about the individual.

A shop steward should consider every gripe or minor complaint from any of his constituents, no matter who presents it or how unimportant it may seem. Otherwise a grievance which could have been prevented may develop.

Important Points

1. Stewards, like supervisors, should avoid favoritism.
2. They should be consistent in processing grievances of all employees they represent.
3. They should try to avoid bias against those they dislike.
4. They should not favor friends.

Failure to Set a Good Example

A shop steward should set a good example for the employees he represents. If he does not, he will probably be responsible for causing grievances. If a steward violates company rules, goofs off on the job, or in any other way sets a bad example, employees are likely to follow his bad example and cause trouble which can be expected to result in grievances. The steward who opposes every move on the part of the foreman or who is overly aggressive in his dealings with the foreman can also cause grievances. Employees are inclined to follow the steward's lead; hence the steward should try to set a good example. He must learn to be tactful and diplomatic in his dealings with the foreman.

Important Points

1. A steward should set a good example for the employees.
2. He should abide by company rules, and strictly follow the contract provisions, as employees look to him for leadership.

Playing Union Politics

Sometimes an ambitious shop steward, anxious to impress his union supervisors, may do things which cause grievances. For example, he may actually stir up grievances in his department in order to show the union officers that he is doing a good job for the union members. He may not realize that the quantity of grievances he processes is not nearly as important as his judgment in handling justified complaints and formal grievances. This does not imply, however, that he should fail to point out to a worker that he has a justified grievance, if he discovers that the employee has one. Sometimes an employee does not realize that he has a grievance, and if the steward discovers that he has, he should offer to help him.

Important Points

1. Stewards should avoid stirring up grievances for political purposes, but should not fail to process any justified complaints or grievances.
2. The quantity of grievances a steward handles is relatively unimportant; his manner of processing them is very important.

Allowing Rumors to Circulate

Stewards, like supervisors, should try to counteract unfounded rumors. In fact, the steward can sometimes squelch rumors more easily than the supervisor can, because he probably will hear the rumor before the supervisor does. Rumors produce apprehension and uncertainty on the part of employees, which frequently result in grievances.

When a steward hears a rumor, he should investigate it to determine the facts. This may involve discussing the rumor with the supervisor. After he obtains the facts, he should give them to the employees. The steward and the foreman working together can often be most effective in dispelling rumors. Rumors unless they are counteracted by facts can cause grievances.

Important Point

Stewards, like supervisors, should investigate any rumor to determine the facts, which should then be explained to the employees.

3 | Recognizing and Preventing Causes of Grievances

Many grievances can be anticipated and prevented by intelligent supervisors and shop stewards who understand the basic principles of human relations. They must appreciate the benefits to all concerned of preventing grievances, and must have the patience to try to do so. One goal of every supervisor and shop steward should be to try to eliminate causes of grievances whenever possible.

This chapter discusses principles which, if properly applied, should prevent most grievances from developing.

PREGRIEVANCE PATTERNS OF EMPLOYEE BEHAVIOR

An alert supervisor can frequently detect changes in the behavioral pattern of an employee, or group of employees, which foretell an impending grievance. An employee's shop steward can probably detect changes in an employee's attitude and actions before the foreman does, because the steward usually has closer contact with employees.

Changes in an employee's behavior such as the following indicate that something is seriously disturbing him (or her):

1. Loss of interest in the work;

2. Adverse change in attitude toward the job, fellow workers, supervisor, the department, or the company;

3. Less willingness to cooperate;

4. Increased absenteeism;
5. Decreased quality or quantity of work produced;
6. More time spent away from work station;
7. Tendency toward antagonism and nonacceptance of supervisor's authority.

This list is not complete, but it indicates the types of behavioral change to which the supervisor and the steward should be alert.

Examples of Pregrievance Behavior

One case in which an alert supervisor averted a grievance is described below:

• Joe Wells had been a drill-press operator for 10 years in a company which manufactured automotive components. He had always been a steady, dependable worker, and was well liked by the other men, although he was quiet and retiring. He had a good relationship with his foreman. In fact, the foreman had sometimes asked him to break in a newly hired man so he, the foreman, could tend to other important duties. Joe considered these men as "his boys" and they regarded Joe much as they would an older brother.

The foreman noticed, however, that Joe had been gradually losing interest in his job over a six-month period. The quality and quantity of his work were dropping off, and he was away from his drill press more frequently than usual, even though he was working on a piecework basis.

The foreman was concerned, and finally decided to talk to Joe in an attempt to ascertain the reason for the change. After a couple of discussions, the foreman sensed that Joe was no longer getting sufficient satisfaction from his work and felt his work was no longer considered as important to the company as it had been in the past. The underlying reasons were as follows:

When Joe Wells had started to work for the company 10 years before, the drill-press department had consisted of only

14 men and the foreman. However, the company had prospered and the department had expanded to a total of 30 drill-press operators. Other changes had been made in the department, too. A little less than a year earlier, management had appointed a man to make all set-ups and sharpen drills for the operators, tasks each man had previously done for himself. It was assumed that the help would be welcomed by the operators.

Before the set-up man was appointed, however, Joe had, on occasion, sharpened drills for "his boys" when they had a burring operation to perform. (It should be noted that grinding a drill for burring use is quite different from grinding it for drilling holes, and requires a special skill.) Joe could do this kind of drill-grinding even better than the set-up man.

The solution to Joe's problem was simple. The foreman called him and the set-up man together and explained that hereafter Joe would make his own set-ups and grind his own tools, since he was well qualified and desired to do so. The set-up man did not object because he had plenty of work to do in servicing the other men. Joe was pleased because his foreman had recognized and appreciated his skill and ability.

This was a situation that could have resulted in a grievance if the foreman had not noticed the change in Joe's behavior and decided to try to find out the reason for it. Joe would probably eventually have voiced a grievance about some other issue, such as not being able to earn as much on piecework as he had previously, or overly tight standards, when actually he was unhappy only because he felt that his job had been downgraded and some of his skill had been considered of little value.

Incidentally, Joe Wells was promoted to set-up man himself a few months later when a second one was needed because of further expansion of the department.

Important Points

Wisely, the foreman had—

1. Discovered that a problem existed;

2. Defined the problem;

3. Identified the cause of the problem; and

4. Acted intelligently and promptly to eliminate the cause of the problem, thus forestalling a grievance.

The following is an example of a case in which a pregrievance behavior change was not investigated in time.

• A salesman in the photo equipment department of a very large department store received excellent ratings for about six years. The store followed a policy of interviewing employees every six months and obtaining evaluations by supervisors. Then, over a period of two years, the store received an increasing number of complaints from customers claiming that the salesman did not wait on them properly or ignored their presence altogether. His evaluation ratings dropped as a result. One day a new supervisor accused the employee of losing some sales slips. The employee went into a blind rage, screamed at the supervisor, then went to the department head and, in front of customers, accused him in a loud and abusive manner of discriminating against him. The employee finally calmed down and went to see a doctor, who gave him a sedative. The employee was discharged, and filed a grievance which was arbitrated. Testimony at the arbitration hearing disclosed that the employee resented the fact that even though he was given excellent ratings for many years, he had been passed over for promotion three times. Moreover, he was requested to teach each of the supervisors the technical knowledge required to sell photographic equipment. It became evident that he manifested his strong resentment against the company by not paying much attention to customers. When the new supervisor accused him, in his opinion falsely, of losing sales slips, his smoldering resentment finally exploded and he behaved in a manner that was out of proportion to the immediate incident.

Important Points

1. The company was not aware of the employee's growing resentment.

2. The personnel office did not investigate the reasons why an employee with excellent ratings for many years should suddenly ignore customers.

Employees' Personal Problems

An employee's change in behavior could, of course, be due to a personal problem not related to his job, such as financial worry, marital difficulty, anxiety about a sick member of his family, or, possibly, his own health. In any case, the supervisor should take steps as diplomatically as possible to determine the cause of the employee's change in behavior, and then do what he can to help the employee overcome his problem. The supervisor should keep in mind that he must deal with the whole person in his relationship with an employee.

If the problem is a personal one, not related to the job, there are several things the supervisor may be able to do to help. Sometimes he can arrange for the employee to obtain help from the personnel department or elsewhere in the company, or from local agencies such as the public health service, specialized medical clinics, a marriage counseling service, or other organization. The supervisor should keep himself informed about agencies of this kind so he can advise employees if the need should arise. Some employees do not realize that service from such organizations is available to them. It is not always possible for the supervisor to help an employee solve personal problems, but at least he can sympathize and offer encouragement.

GUIDELINES FOR SUPERVISORS

A supervisor can prevent grievances, or certainly reduce them to a minimum, by observing the following good basic supervisory practices:

1. Dealing properly with each employee as an individual and a "whole person";

2. Respecting all employees and treating them in a dignified manner;

3. Recognizing superior performance, and giving credit to any employee who makes a good suggestion;

4. Seeking and making an effort to understand the employee's point of view if a problem develops;

5. Being alert to sources of employee irritation;

6. Taking prompt and effective action to eliminate the causes of irritation;

7. Training employees, especially new ones, to do their work properly;

8. Issuing clear orders, with reasons why they are necessary, and making sure the orders are understood;

9. Administering discipline objectively, equitably, and consistently;

10. Enforcing company rules consistently;

11. Avoiding favoritism;

12. Cooperating with the shop steward in eliminating causes of grievances;

13. Knowing provisions of the labor contract.

This list could certainly be expanded, but as it is it indicates some of the steps a supervisor can take to reduce the number of grievances from his employees. The application of these guidelines will be discussed in Chapter 4.

Types of Employees

Probably one of the most difficult problems for a supervisor is to determine the best way to deal with each employee under his supervision. Each has a different temperament, and what is effective in dealing with Bill may be just the wrong method to use in dealing with Art. For instance, Bill may be the volatile, excitable type who gets things off his chest, flaring up and blowing his top at the slightest provocation, and telling the other guy off, sometimes in colorful language. Men like Bill usually calm down quickly after releasing their emotions, and the foreman can then discuss with them the reason for their outburst in a reasonable manner. On the other hand, Art may be the quiet, introspective, serious type who seems always to have control of his emotions and seldom shows any outward evidence that he is displeased. But if Art finally explodes, he is likely to take hours, or even days, to get back to normal.

Of these two extreme types, Bill is the easier one to deal with. The foreman will be aware immediately that Bill has a gripe, and, given a short cooling-off period, he can talk sensibly to him to determine what is bothering him and what to do about it. The foreman must, of course, restrain his own emotions until Bill has cooled off. Art, on the other hand, had probably been brooding about his problem for days, or even weeks, before it overpowered him to the point that he could no longer cope with it by himself. His blow-up may be much more difficult to deal with and will require more patience and skill in handling. The foreman must control his emotions, talk calmly to Art, show sympathy and understanding, avoid criticism, and be patient until Art is ready to talk about his complaint. His cooling-off period will take much longer than Bill's but only after he has regained his composure can the foreman deal effectively with him.

Fortunately, most people are at neither of these extremes. Most are a combination of the two types, some more like Bill, others more like Art. The important thing is for a foreman to know his subordinates as individuals. He must evaluate their personalities and temperaments to know the most effective way to deal with each one.

The foreman should know when and how to use praise to obtain the desired result in dealing with a certain employee. Likewise, he must know whether certain employees would respond more readily to a challenge or to objective criticism. There is no substitute for knowing employees as individuals.

Important Point

A supervisor should realize that he will have to supervise various types of people, and should strive to learn how to deal with each person most effectively as an individual.

Getting to Know Employees

How can a foreman or supervisor get to know his employees? He should maintain close personal contact with them on the job, and also in job-related outside activities. He must have a sincere interest in them and must demonstrate this interest. He should have personal contact with each employee every day on the job. He need not take more than a few minutes with each one, but he should visit each employee at his machine, his bench, or his desk at least once every day, if only to ask how things are going, to inquire about the family's health, or make some other personal contact.

Bowling on the department's team, playing softball with his employees, and other recreational activities are also good ways of getting to know employees. Even if the foreman is not a good bowler, his men will appreciate his joining with them in this activity. In fact, they may be inclined to like him better because some of them can bowl better than he. Even if he doesn't bowl or play softball, the foreman can be an interested spectator and thereby support his men. The important thing is for him to mingle informally with his employees away from the work situation. This will give him the opportunity to know his employees better, and, more important, the employees will learn to know their foreman or supervisor as a person, not just as a boss.

The supervisor should be friendly with all his employees, but should not be too intimate with any of them. Intimacy is likely to cause trouble, because some employees may assume that the supervisor will favor his intimate friends, whether this is true or not. Besides, the supervisor will find it difficult to discipline a close personal friend if it should become necessary.

Important Points

Supervisors should try to get acquainted with their employees in order to learn how to handle each as an individual most effectively. They should strive to be friendly without becoming too intimate.

Treating Employees With Respect and Dignity

There is no better guide for supervisors in dealing with employees than the Golden Rule, "Do to others as you would have others do to you." A supervisor should try to put himself in the other person's shoes when dealing with his employees. He should question himself: "If I were this employee and he were my boss, how would I want him to act?" This will impress on the supervisor not only the necessity of being fair, honest, and considerate, but also that he should respect the employee's dignity as an individual in all dealings with him. This is the way people want to be treated by others at all times.

Recognizing Superior Performance of Employees

An employee who does a better-than-normal job deserves his supervisor's commendation. A pat on the back for a job well done will usually have a beneficial effect. The employee will appreciate the fact that his supervisor has recognized his extra effort. Without a compliment from his supervisor, the employee will not know whether the supervisor is aware of his extra effort, and may conclude that since it is not appreciated, he might as well go back to working like the people who are doing just an average or mediocre job. It is important also for a supervisor to give credit to an employee who makes a good suggestion.

Understanding the Employee's Point of View

A supervisor should not jump to conclusions, but should talk with the employee, ask questions, and listen intently and sympathetically. If an employee does not express himself as well as could be desired, it is the supervisor who must make sure that they are, in fact, communicating properly. He must assure himself that he understands the problem from the employee's point of view. Only then can he separate facts from opinions and decide what action he should take.

Determining True Causes of Dissatisfaction

The supervisor should realize that the employee may consciously or unconsciously disguise the real cause of his dissatisfaction. An employee may give the impression that he thinks he is underpaid for the job he is doing, when actually he is worried about an impending financial problem such as a serious, unexpected illness in his family. Or he may complain that his machine does not operate properly, when he is really not using the correct technique. Unless the supervisor determines the true cause of the problem, he cannot take the most effective action to help the employee.

Eliminating Sources of Irritation

The supervisor who has gained his employees' confidence and let them see that he is friendly and fair will find that they will come to him for help when they have problems or complaints instead of just griping to fellow workers. And they will come to him before their problems become exaggerated.

A supervisor should never be offended when an employee or the shop steward comes to him with a gripe about something which irritates him. On the contrary, he should be glad he has learned about the employee's displeasure so he can check into the matter and take corrective action. A minor complaint should not be neglected, since it may be the forerunner of a major grievance. It has been said that most fires could have been put out with a cupful of water if detected soon enough. Similarly, a potential grievance can usually be averted if the cause of dissatisfaction is discovered and eliminated soon enough.

Important Points

A supervisor is likely to avert a developing grievance if he does the following after detecting a change in an employee's behavior:

1. Determines the cause of the employee's dissatisfaction;
2. Seeks and understands the employee's point of view;
3. Discusses the problem with the employee unemotionally and objectively;
4. Takes prompt action to eliminate the cause of irritation.

Training Employees

Many employee complaints and grievances stem from misunderstandings between the employee and the supervisor. Misunderstandings frequently are caused by insufficient or inadequate training by the supervisor. This is especially true if the employee is newly hired or inexperienced in the type of work he must do. Even if the employee has had similar experience elsewhere, a certain amount of training is necessary before he can adapt his skill to his job in a new company.

• For example, an experienced punch-press operator who had been hired about a year before had an accident which broke an expensive forming die. The foreman disciplined him severely for using an unacceptable method of operating the punch press. During the grievance proceedings which followed this incident, it was brought out that the foreman had not instructed his employee regarding this operation. He had assumed that the man would know how to perform the operation properly because he had had many years of experience. However, the operation was quite different than any the man had performed previously. He did not want to ask the foreman how to do the job since this, he felt, would expose his ignorance. Also, he had observed another operator who used the same faulty technique on the same operation without getting into trouble. Who was at fault? Obviously, both the employee and his foreman shared the blame for the accident. The operator should have asked for proper instructions, but the foreman was even more to blame than the operator. He should have made certain that this man knew exactly how the operation should be performed, and should have been aware that another operator had been performing the operation incorrectly.

A supervisor must always take definite steps to be sure that an employee understands exactly what he is expected to do, and train him to do it properly if he does not know. Training employees is very important, especially for new employees.

Important Points

1. The supervisor must always take definite steps to be sure that an employee understands exactly what he is expected to do.
2. All new employees, even those who have considerable job experience, should be given some training, to ensure that they can perform each operation in the way the supervisor prefers.

Job Training for Employees

Much time, thought, and attention have since been given to the problem of effective training, but the basic principles were developed by Training Within Industry Service (TWI), an adjunct of the United States War Manpower Commission, in the early 1940s. TWI developed a four-step procedure called Job Instruction Training (JIT), which is still the most effective training procedure devised specifically for use in industry. The four steps are as follows:

1. *Preparation*

    a. *Prepare to instruct.* The instructor (foreman) must know exactly what he plans to teach and how he will do it. He must have readily available all necessary tools, equipment in good working condition, blueprints, operation sheets, and so forth.

    b. *Prepare the learner.* Put him at ease. Explain the job briefly and find out what he already knows about it. Arouse his interest in learning the job. Place him in the best position to observe how the job is to be performed.

2. *Present the Operation*
Tell, show, and illustrate one important step at a time. Stress each key point. Instruct clearly, completely, and patiently, but no more than the learner can comprehend. Repeat the demonstration if necessary. Make sure the learner understands and is ready to try the operation himself.

3. *Try Out Performance*
Have the learner perform the operation. Correct his errors but avoid being too critical. Have him explain each key point as he does the job. Make sure he understands. Continue until the instructor knows the learner can perform the operation correctly. Tell him that his efforts are appreciated, and compliment him if he does well.

4. *Followup*
Have the learner do the job on his own. Check frequently to ascertain that he has encountered no problems. Encourage questions. Repeat instructions diplomatically, if necessary. Continue to check his progress from time to time until he has obviously mastered the job.

Issuing Orders to Employees

Related to giving proper instructions to employees is the issuing of orders. Each order, whether verbal or written, should be clear, and the supervisor should make sure that it is understood by the employee or employees to whom it is given. He should include the reason or reasons why the order is necessary. A story will illustrate this point.

• A construction foreman told Walt to "Dig a hole about two feet wide, six feet long, and five feet deep." Walt worked hard in the hot sun, completed the job, and called the foreman when he had finished digging. The foreman took a casual look and told Walt to fill it up, then dig a similar hole a few feet away. Walt was baffled but did as his foreman told him to do. Again Walt called the foreman to inspect the hole. The foreman looked in the hole, then repeated his instruction to shovel the dirt back into the hole and dig another one. Walt looked at his foreman and then exploded. "Boss, you're crazy. Dig a hole, fill it up. Dig another hole, fill it up. You don't know what you're doing. I quit." The foreman then explained to Walt that there was a sewer pipe about four feet below the surface in the general vicinity and that it was important to locate it before he could let the bulldozer operator work in the area. Walt's reaction was, "Why didn't you tell me, boss? OK, I'll dig until I find it."

Giving Orders Properly

It is not enough for a supervisor to give an order; he should explain the reason, or reasons, why the order is necessary. Employees want to know that the work they do serves a useful purpose. They need to feel that they are making a significant contribution in addition to getting paid for the work they perform. Man does not live by bread alone.

Orders should be stated in simple, concise language, but completely and accurately. This is the best way to make them clear to those concerned. The use of unusual words or complicated sentence structure may cause confusion. President Lincoln's famous Gettysburg Address is a good example of simple words and short sentences. Everyone in his audience, and millions of schoolchildren who have since read this speech, understand what President Lincoln said on this occasion. Wordiness should be avoided. Brevity is desirable for easy comprehension by the one who receives the order. However, completeness and accuracy should not be sacrificed for conciseness.

An order should be worded in a positive but objective manner as something required by the job, rather than as an arrogant command from the supervisor. If an employee does not understand an order completely, his questions should be answered. In fact, the supervisor should take the initiative to ensure that his order is clearly understood. He should ask the employee to tell him what the order means to him if it is a complicated one.

Involved or complicated orders, and those which affect a group of employees, are best put in writing. Sometimes an order issued to a group should be discussed with the group to give all members an opportunity to ask questions. This will ensure that all have the same understanding.

The supervisor should appeal to the self-interest of the recipient if an order provides any benefit to him. For example, an order which requires observance of a safety rule is issued to protect the individual as well as the company. The supervisor should emphasize the value to the employees of obeying the rule.

Important Points

1. Orders should be clear and concise, but given in enough detail to convey them accurately.
2. Complicated orders and those involving several employees should be written out.
3. The reason for an order should be stated.

Administering Discipline Fairly, Objectively, and Consistently

Employees, like all people, resent injustice. Most people have a fair sense of justice, and an employee will usually know when he deserves to be disciplined. However, he will resent unfair discipline, that is, discipline more severe than his offense should justify. Also, he will resent being disciplined more severely than a fellow worker for the same offense.

If an employee commits an offense, the supervisor should not ignore it. He should ascertain the facts, determine the reason, consider the employee's previous record, and check into any extenuating circumstances, prior offenses by the employee, discipline imposed on others for the same or a similar offense, and so forth. Then and only then is the supervisor in a position to decide objectively and without anger what the proper disciplinary action should be. It may be only a verbal warning, or it may be a written warning, disciplinary suspension, or even discharge. It is very important that the punishment fit the offense.

A supervisor must not impose discipline when he is angry. He must delay until he can consider all the facts and make an objective decision. It is essential, too, that he be consistent in administering discipline to all his employees. If he suspends John for three days without pay, whereas he gave Henry only a written warning last week for the same offense, he is asking for trouble unless John's past record is bad and Henry's is his first offense. Judgment must be used in each discipline case.

Enforcing Company Rules

Enforcing company rules usually involves some sort of disciplinary action by the supervisor, even though it may be no more than a verbal reprimand. Rules must be enforced fairly and consistently. For example, if there is a rule against smoking in the department or in a specified area, it must be consistently enforced, and each employee who violates it must be disciplined in the same way. Otherwise, an employee who is more severely disciplined than another will have a justified grievance. Most important, the supervisor must never violate a rule himself. Any inconsistency in the enforcement of company rules leads to employee dissatisfaction and a belief that the supervisor is guilty of favoritism.

It is not only important for each supervisor to enforce company rules consistently within his department, but rules should be enforced consistently by all supervisors throughout the company. This means that supervisors should keep higher management informed regarding rule violations so management can control the administration of discipline for violations. If penalties for rule violations are specified in a union contract, it is imperative that there be no deviation from them. A supervisor should inform his superior immediately about any rule violation, and ask advice regarding the company's policy if there is any question about the penalty to be imposed.

Important Point

Supervisors should enforce company rules impartially and consistently.

Avoiding Favoritism

A supervisor must guard against showing favoritism to any of his employees. Most supervisors appreciate that they must not discriminate against any employee, but many fail to realize that granting favors to individual employees is a form of discrimination against the others. Favoritism results in envy and jealousy, and destroys employees' confidence and respect for the supervisor. Morale breaks down, the disfavored employees become discouraged, and teamwork within the department is disrupted.

Avoiding favoritism is difficult even for the supervisor who sincerely wants to do so. Everyone is instinctively attracted to certain people and repelled by others. A supervisor may not be aware that he favors some employees because he likes them as individuals, or that he treats some unfairly because he dislikes them. He must guard against this human trait. He must continually remind himself to avoid assigning the easy jobs to the employees he likes and the tough jobs to those whose personalities do not appeal to him. He must grant no favors and make no promises to any employee that he would not give to any other.

If a supervisor is objective and honest with himself as well as others, he will realize that the employee he dislikes may be as good or better a worker than those he likes better, and therefore deserves a square deal. One thing is certain: employees will be immediately aware of any evidence of favoritism. They are very sensitive to this form of injustice, and will recognize it before the supervisor does if he makes this kind of mistake.

Important Point

Supervisors must not show favoritism. All employees should be treated alike, even though it may be difficult to act the same toward an employee who is disliked and one who is liked personally.

Cooperating with the Shop Steward

An effective way to eliminate the causes of grievances is for the foreman to cooperate with the shop steward. This statement may not be believed by some supervisors, who feel that stewards have caused them trouble in the past. A supervisor who feels this way should search his soul to discover whether he may not be at least partially responsible. How has he treated the steward? Has he, as well as the steward, had a chip on his shoulder? Does he accept the fact that the steward also has a job to do? Has he looked beyond the steward's militant and possibly disagreeable actions to discover his true motives? Good supervisors and good stewards want harmonious relationships within the department. They have much more in common than in conflict, especially in their desire to eliminate the causes of grievances.

The supervisor should realize that the shop steward usually is aware of any condition or incident which irritates the employees before he himself knows about it. The steward is part of the work force. He is closer to the employees than the foreman can ever be, since he is one of them and the foreman is part of management. An employee will usually tell his troubles to his steward before the foreman has any inkling that he is dissatisfied.

If the steward reports any kind of employee dissatisfaction to the foreman, the foreman should listen carefully. He should not take offense, even if the problem reflects discredit on him, or if the steward is undiplomatic in his criticism. Actually, the foreman should be grateful that the steward has pointed out the trouble, thus giving him a chance to take proper action. The foreman must realize that he, not the steward, is the one who has authority to act in eliminating the causes of dissatisfaction. The steward has done all he can do, usually, by reporting the problem.

The foreman should weigh objectively what he has learned from the steward. He must then decide the proper thing to do and take prompt action. He may find it desirable, or even necessary, to confer with his superior before making his decision. He should not make a hasty decision, but must come up with a prompt answer after considering all angles of the problem. In all such cases, he should report back to the steward regarding his decision and the action he proposes to take.

Often the foreman should ask the steward to convey his decision to the employee or employees concerned. The foreman should realize that sometimes employees will accept his decision more readily if they know that their steward approves of it, and especially if they feel that he has had some part in developing it. This does not detract from the supervisor's authority in any way, nor does it cause the employees to lose respect for him. On the contrary, they are likely to be impressed with his open-mindedness and integrity. The supervisor should strive for smooth and efficient operation of his department, not for glory as a big-shot boss. It does not detract from the foreman's position to give the steward credit for his assistance either. If deserved credit is given to the steward, he will probably be even more cooperative in the future. The foreman's superiors are concerned primarily with results obtained by the department, so the foreman who gets good results with help from his steward will be given full credit by management.

Some of the viewpoints expressed above may seem unrealistic to those supervisors who have had unpleasant experiences in their dealings with shop stewards. But accepting the steward as an ally has been successful in many cases, and this approach can be made to work well in other difficult situations if the foreman has sufficient patience and tries hard enough.

Important Points

1. A cooperative relationship between the supervisor and the shop steward will produce better results for employees as well as the company.
2. Both the supervisor and the steward should strive to respect each other's position and work together toward the solution of mutual problems.

Knowing Provisions of Labor Contract

It is very important for the supervisor to know in detail the provisions of the collective bargaining agreement. By knowing it he will avoid violating it himself and can also cite specific provisions to the shop steward.

The supervisor has the responsibility of studying the provisions of the contract and following them. However, certain provisions of the contract may be subject to different interpretations.

In one instance the managers of five quarries owned by the same company operated under the same collective bargaining agreement but interpreted its provisions differently, which gave rise to many grievances. The company then engaged a consultant to meet with the managers and develop a uniform interpretation for each provision. Thereafter the number of grievances was considerably reduced.

GUIDELINES FOR SHOP STEWARDS

Just as a supervisor can take steps to prevent or reduce the number of grievances, a shop steward also can take effective steps to eliminate the causes of grievances. Some of these steps are the same as those recommended for supervisors, but there are some differences. Suggested guidelines are:

1. Dealing with each person as an individual;

2. Respecting employees and the supervisor, and treating them in a dignified manner;

3. Seeking and understanding the employee's and the supervisor's point of view;

4. Being alert to sources of employee irritation;

5. Investigating and evaluating each gripe to determine whether it is justified; convincing the employee, if possible, when it is not justified;

6. Reporting justified gripes and irritations to the foreman; following up to ensure that he takes prompt action;

7. Reporting back to employees to keep them informed regarding action on their complaints;

8. Avoiding favoritism;

9. Cooperating with the foreman in eliminating the causes of grievances.

This is not a complete list, but it does suggest some of the ways a shop steward can help reduce the number of grievances.

Getting to Know Employees

A shop steward must get to know each of the employees he represents, just as a foreman must know his employees as individuals. This is usually no problem for the steward because he is one of them. He is in close personal contact with them every day and soon learns how to deal effectively with each one as a person. He should, however, be aware of how to deal with the different types of people.

The steward should take the initiative in getting to know new employees and in gaining their confidence. To accomplish this, he must be sincere, considerate, and helpful to them in every way he can. He should encourage them to come to him if they have any questions or problems which they cannot resolve for themselves, or which the foreman has been unable to resolve satisfactorily.

Not only should the steward get to know the employees, he should get to know his foreman as a person, too. In fact, he should know the personnel director and other members of management with whom he has contacts as individuals, and he should know his union officers as individuals also.

Important Points

1. A shop steward, like a supervisor, should get to know each employee he represents personally.
2. Especially with a new employee, the steward should take the initiative in becoming acquainted and should make a sincere effort to gain the employee's confidence.

Treating People with Respect and Dignity

The Golden Rule applies to shop steward as well as to supervisors. The steward may find it fairly easy to be considerate of employees, and to treat them with respect and dignity. He may find this more difficult in his dealings with the supervisor or foreman, but he must remember that all people deserve to be treated decently, and that their dignity as human beings should be respected.

A steward should not bypass the supervisor in processing a grievance. He should always check with the supervisor before leaving his job to investigate an employee's complaint; most collective bargaining agreements specify this requirement. The steward should avoid name-calling, and he should not rub it in when he is proved to be right and the supervisor wrong. Letting the other fellow save face will pay dividends in future dealings with each other. He and the supervisor should both strive to determine what is right, not who is wrong.

Important Points

1. A shop steward should remember that the supervisor should be treated decently, and must respect his supervisor's dignity as a person.
2. He should work with the supervisor to determine what is right, not who is to blame.

Understanding the Employee's Point of View

Shop stewards, like foremen, should avoid hasty conclusions about employee's complaints. A steward should listen carefully to the employee who has a gripe, but he must sometimes search for the real cause of the employee's dissatisfaction, which the employee himself may not recognize. The steward should ask the employee questions to get all the facts, and must be sure that he understands what the employee is trying to convey to him.

Sometimes there may have been incidents which occurred prior to the one which triggered the employee's gripe. The steward should, in most cases, talk with other people in addition to the one who filed the complaint, in order to get complete understanding of the problem before deciding what action he should take.

Important Points

1. A steward should make a conscious effort to understand the employee's point of view.
2. Sometimes he may have to probe for the true cause of a grievance.
3. He should avoid making a decision until he is certain he fully comprehends the employee's viewpoint.

Eliminating Sources of Irritation

Too much importance cannot be placed on the desirability of eliminating the sources of grievances. The ability of a shop steward and his foreman or supervisor to eliminate the causes of grievances will be recognized and appreciated by union officials and management alike. This, together with equitable solutions in the first step of formal grievances which do arise, is the core of successful labor relations so far as the steward and the foreman are concerned. It is far better to eliminate causes than to resolve grievances.

Stewards must usually enlist help from foremen to eliminate sources of grievances. It is possible, in rare cases, for the steward to eliminate causes of grievances, especially if the cause is a misunderstanding or other unreal situation. Generally, the steward can be effective only by seeking the foreman's help.

Important Points

1. Stewards, as well as supervisors, should do all they can to help eliminate sources of irritation which are likely to cause grievances.
2. Frequently a steward becomes aware of such conditions before the supervisor does, and if so, he should immediately call it to the supervisor's attention.

Investigating and Evaluating Employees' Complaints

A steward should investigate each gripe or irritating situation to determine what action he should take. In addition to listening to the employee and searching for the true cause of his problem, he should question other employees, and he should then evaluate the problem. If his analysis shows that the employee's gripe is unjustified, he should try to convince the employee that he does not have a justified complaint. On the other hand, if there is reason to believe it may be justified, he should convey the employee's viewpoint to the foreman immediately, if there is nothing he can do to alleviate the problem.

Important Point

1. Before taking action, a steward should investigate an employee's complaint or grievance.

2. If it appears justified, he should convey it to the supervisor; if unjustified, he should explain why to the employee.

Reporting Justified Complaints to Supervisor and Following Them Up

If the employee or group are justified in their displeasure about an irritating situation, the steward should convey their dissatisfaction to the supervisor or foreman immediately. He should give him all the information he has obtained from the employee or employees concerned. He should use all proper methods possible to get the supervisor to act, if action must come from management to eliminate the cause of dissatisfaction. He should make it clear that he, the steward, is ready and willing to cooperate in the elimination of the irritating situation. He should also follow up to ensure that management, through the supervisor, takes effective action to resolve the problem.

Keeping Employees Informed About Action Taken

A steward must keep the employees informed about what has been done to resolve their complaints. If the problem is one which the supervisor must refer to higher levels of management for settlement, the steward should tell the employees this rather than letting them think the foreman has failed to act. But the steward should follow up through frequent contacts with his foreman, until an answer is given. The steward should appreciate that some employee's complaints require a management decision which the foreman has no authority to make, especially if company policy is affected or if substantial expenditures are involved to correct the trouble. The steward should also keep his union officers informed at all stages.

Important Points

1. When processing a justified grievance, the steward should be as persuasive as possible in a nonmilitant way, and should follow-up as necessary to get action.

2. He should keep the employee informed regarding the status of the proceedings, and should also inform his union officers.

Avoiding Favoritism

It would be unusual if the shop steward, like the supervisor, did not have favorites. Stewards, like all people, prefer some employees to others, but this must not influence them to go to bat for a friend whose complaint lacks merit, or to neglect to process a less esteemed employee's justified one. Favoritism on the part of a steward can be as destructive of morale as favoritism by the foreman. The good shop steward will avoid showing any evidence of favoritism to any of his union members, just as a good foreman will avoid favoritism. It may be even harder for a steward to avoid favoritism than for a foreman, but he must do so if he is to protect his position as an impartial representative of the employees. Again, *what* is right is much more important than *who* is right.

Important Point

Stewards, like supervisors, must avoid favoritism. They must be impartial in giving service both to those they dislike and those who are personal friends.

Cooperating with the Foreman

A shop steward has much to gain by cooperating with his foreman in eliminating the causes of grievances. He should realize that the foreman has his job to do and that sometimes this will bring the steward and foreman into conflict, or at least into disagreement. But the two have much more in common than in conflict so far as avoiding and settling grievances is concerned.

The steward must have patience with his foreman in cases over which the foreman does not have control. If the foreman is sincerely trying to eliminate causes of grievances and is doing all he can reasonably be expected to do, he deserves the steward's confidence. Working together in a spirit of goodwill, they can be effective in eliminating causes and settling grievances.

Reference has been made to the need for proper employee training in order to prevent misunderstandings which can lead to grievances. Proper training also helps to give an employee confidence in his ability to do his work. An employee with self-confidence is less likely to become dissatisfied than one who lacks this inner feeling of security.

In addition to job training for employees, progress toward eliminating causes of grievances can be made by training supervisors and shop stewards in basic human relations. Middle and top management and union officials, also, can benefit from this type of training.

Important Point

The steward should keep in mind that causes of grievances can be best eliminated by cooperation with the supervisor; grievances are a problem they have in common.

GUIDELINES FOR TOP MANAGEMENT

When a person is selected to fill a top management post, his responsibility for the effective functioning of the company is broadened, and includes better labor relations. The following are a few guidelines which may be helpful:

1. Select foremen and supervisors with potential to handle people as well as technical competence.
2. Provide intensive training courses for new supervisors and periodic refresher courses.
3. Establish good personnel policies and practices.
4. Create climate for good human relations throughout company.
5. Explain new contract provisions.

6. Set up periodic conferences during which top management can discuss new concepts in employee relations.

Select Foremen and Supervisors With Potential to Handle People

Management usually selects foremen and supervisors on the basis of their technical competence. The best tool and die maker or best bookkeeper is usually selected to fill a supervisory position.

Although it is very important for the supervisor to be technically competent, his supervisory functions require more than technical knowledge. When a person becomes a supervisor, the nature of his duties changes. He is now required to handle personnel problems. If the plant is unionized, he must also deal with the shop steward on a day-to-day basis and apply the provisions of the collective bargaining agreement.

Top management usually assumes that the best tool and die maker or best bookkeeper will also have the skills to supervise people, but experience has shown that this is not a safe assumption. The ability to handle people involves the use of skills which are quite different. It is unusual to find people who, in addition to being technically competent, are also competent to handle the labor relations and personnel functions of a supervisory job.

Important Point

Top management should select supervisors who have the labor relations and personnel skills necessary to perform their nontechnical duties in addition to technical knowledge and expertise. If they have these skills, grievances can be prevented.

Training for Supervisors

Each prospective supervisor should take an intensive supervisory training course and also periodic refresher courses. Learning how to handle people is sometimes more difficult than learning how to operate a machine, and requires much time. It often requires unlearning wrong attitudes and habits.

Training Within Industry Service developed a good basic program of human relations training for supervisors, called "Job Relations Training." Its four-step program for dealing with employee relations problems is as follows:

1. *Get the Facts*
   Review the record. Find out what company rules and practices apply. Talk with individuals concerned. Get opinions and feelings. Be sure to get the whole story.

2. *Weigh and Decide*
   Distinguish between facts and opinions. Consider their bearing on each other. Fit the evidence together. Check practices and policies. Decide what actions are possible. Consider the effect of each action on individuals, the group, and on production. Don't jump to a conclusion.

3. *Take Action*
   Should the supervisor handle this problem himself, or does he need help? Should he refer this problem to his superior? Consider the timing of action to be taken. But act, don't pass the buck.

4. *Check Results*
   How soon should the supervisor follow up? How often should he check? Watch for changes in production, attitudes, and relationships. Did the action which was taken help? If not, what action should be taken?

Since supervisors get results through other people, they should be trained further to realize that good employee relations depend upon the following rules:

1. Let each employee know how he is getting along. Let each one know what is expected of him. Point out ways he can improve.

2. Give credit when due. Look for extra or unusual performance, and recognize it by telling the employee at once that it has been noticed and appreciated.

3. Tell people in advance about changes which will affect them. Tell them why the change is necessary. Get them to accept the change if possible.

4. Make the best use of each employee's ability. Look for skill and ability not now being used. Never stand in an employee's way. Treat people as individuals.

Probably the best method of training supervisors is by means of group conferences. Each group should be limited to about 15 participants, and a specific subject should be discussed at each meeting. A qualified leader should be in charge of each group meeting to introduce the subject and to encourage all members of the group to participate in the discussion. Most progressive large and medium-sized companies already hold such training sessions, but smaller companies also should have this kind of program.

If the company is unionized, one or more sessions for each group of supervisors should be devoted to the interpretation and discussion of any newly negotiated contract. This will help all supervisors to understand contract provisions which affect their operations, and all supervisors will get the same interpretation. The leader of such conferences should be the personnel director or other member of management who participated in the contract negotiations.

Some companies have found joint meetings with supervisors and shop stewards to discuss a new contract quite effective. This tends to clarify misunderstandings between foremen and stewards regarding each of their rights and restrictions. If joint meetings are held, usually the personnel director and a union officer serve as cochairmen. Whether or not joint meetings should be held depends upon the general relationship between the company and the union.

Good Personnel Policies and Practices

To avoid multiple grievances and the resulting erosion in productivity, top management should set up a personnel department staffed by qualified persons to formulate and administer
sound personnel policies. It should be emphasized that if the
staff members have had no formal training in personnel administration, they will probably not succeed. Too frequently those
in charge of personnel administration are not qualified. In one
company the son of the owner, who was a fighter pilot, was
designated personnel manager; in another, it was the local
high school football hero. In both cases their ineptitude in handling personnel problems caused many grievances that were
submitted to arbitration. In a third case a retired detective was
placed in charge of the personnel office, but he had the intelligence to recognize his shortcomings and immediately took
college courses in personnel administration.

Even if a person has several degrees and is an engineer or
accountant, or is a college professor with a doctorate, it cannot
be assumed that he is competent to administer personnel problems or supervise other people.

Good Human Relations

In the past 30 years much research has been done by industrial
psychologists to determine how best to utilize human resources. They have found that when employees are resentful
because of an inequitable wage structure, favoritism, bad working conditions, or arbitrary hiring, layoff, or discharge practices, they are usually less productive. Job satisfaction is often
more important to an employee than his level of wages and
makes for a more productive employee.

Although most of the largest and most profitable corpora-
tions, such as IBM, General Motors, Union Carbide, and Standard Oil, maintain personnel departments that are staffed by
qualified people who administer sound personnel policies,
there are still many companies who follow the traditional pat-

tern of permitting foremen who have no skills in handling people to make critical personnel decisions and then supporting these decisions even though it is obvious that they were wrong. Conditions like these result in industrial unrest and lower productivity.

Any textbook in personnel administration which covers such topics as job evaluation, wage and salary structures, merit rating, and so forth is a source of good personnel policies and practices.

Most personnel policies and practices are based on good human relations. If top management announces its support for good personnel policies and practices and good human relations, this will set an example that will be followed by subordinates, thus creating the kind of climate which will result in greater job satisfaction, greater productivity, and a lower incidence of grievances.

Important Point

Grievances are likely to occur unless management has established sound, equitable personnel policies which are administered by well-trained, qualified personnel people.

Explain Contract Provisions

If top management wants to prevent grievances, it must conduct periodic conferences for managers, supervisors, and foremen to consider in detail each provision of the collective bargaining agreement. Since many provisions are subject to varying interpretations, it is top management's responsibility to inform its representatives on how they should interpret and apply the contract.

In addition, management should distribute all arbitration awards which interpret the contract, and should maintain a library containing books on personnel administration and arbitration awards such as those published by the Bureau of National Affairs, and encourage foremen, supervisors, and managers to use it.

When a new contract is signed, it is especially important for top management to call a conference of those representatives who are required to administer the contract to discuss its provisions. The conferees should be encouraged to ask questions to avoid any misunderstanding.

Important Point

1. All management representatives must understand the various provisions of the labor contract, and all must interpret these uniformly.

2. Meetings of supervisors are desirable to discuss the contract and review their operations within its provisions.

3. It is especially necessary for management to explain the provisions of each new contract signed with the union to all supervisors.

Training for Higher Levels of Management

Middle and top management can also benefit from training in human relations and how to make sound personnel decisions. All management people are affected, directly or indirectly, by employee relations in their companies. A company's executives and middle management personnel control the climate in their company more than the first-line supervisors. If desirable attitudes of cooperation, fairness, and good will are established at top levels, they will filter down to the first-level supervisors who must put them into effect. Foremen cannot be expected to observe good employee relations practices in the absence of proper management attitudes. They will almost inevitably reflect top-management thinking.

People in top management, therefore, need to question themselves from time to time regarding their attitudes and policies toward all employees, including managerial personnel. This may require an occasional conference of top-level people to discuss employee relations problems. At such a conference, the company's recent experience in personnel problems, grievances, labor turnover, absenteeism, and so forth should be reviewed, as well as suggestions from union representatives. This does not mean that there should be a soft or paternalistic approach; the approach should rather be fair, honest, and sympathetic. Management must let all members of the organization—supervisors, employees, and union representatives—know that it is anxious to eliminate, as far as possible, any condition which causes dissatisfaction on the part of employees. Management can do this effectively by establishing fair policies and ensuring that they are put into effect.

4 | Adjusting Grievances

As we have already discussed, a supervisor's success depends primarily upon his technical knowledge of the work and his ability to obtain results through other people, his subordinates. The latter skill is just as important as technical know-how, and is more difficult to acquire. Most foremen have adequate knowledge about the technical details of the job before they are appointed, or they can learn what they need to know in a relatively short time. Ability to deal effectively with employees and to stimulate them to do their best work, however, is more demanding of the supervisor. Acquisition of this art is worthy of his best efforts. In addition to following the suggestions in previous chapters regarding interpersonal relationships with employees and others, the successful supervisor must become competent in the handling of formal grievances which may develop.

A shop steward's most important function is to help union members in settling their grievances. The steward advises, guides, and serves as spokesman for any member who has a grievance. The ability to deal effectively with people at various levels in the company is, therefore, as important to the steward as to the supervisor.

It should be stressed that the best way to handle grievances is to prevent them from occurring by eliminating the causes of dissatisfaction. However, this ideal is not always attained, and therefore this chapter will outline the basic principles which have proved effective in resolving grievances.

Guidelines for supervisors and for stewards will be outlined separately, although they have much in common.

GUIDING PRINCIPLES FOR SUPERVISORS

Obviously a supervisor must know his company's established grievance procedure, and must abide by its provisions. This procedure tells him what to do, but does not give him much help in how to do it properly. The following basic principles have been found to be effective in adjusting grievances.

1. Listen carefully, with sincere interest. Search for what the employee is trying to say. Be alert to detect the real cause of his grievance if he does not bring it out clearly.

2. Put the grievant at ease. Make it as easy as possible for him to get his grievance off his chest. Do not interrupt him. Be patient.

3. Discuss the problem with him calmly and with an open mind. Avoid arguments. Do not antagonize him.

4. Get his story straight. Get all the facts. Ask logical questions to clarify any doubtful points. Distinguish between facts and opinions.

5. Consider the grievant's viewpoint. Do not assume he is wrong. → false assumption \

6. Avoid snap judgment. Do not jump to a conclusion. Investigate the grievance further by talking with others who may be able to supply pertinent information.

7. Evaluate all facts and opinions before reaching a decision. Be willing to admit mistakes, if any have been made. Give the grievant the benefit of any doubt.

8. Make an equitable decision, then give it to the grievant promptly. Do not pass the buck. If the decision is unfavorable to the grievant, be considerate. Help him to save face if possible.

9. Impose discipline appropriate to the individual situation.

10. Communicate the decision at the appropriate time in the procedure, being as tactful yet direct as possible.

Each of these principles is discussed in more detail below.

Listening to a Grievance

Probably the most important thing a supervisor should learn about the handling of grievances is to listen properly. The importance of listening has been appreciated for thousands of years. Five thousand years ago an Egyptian ruler, Ptah Hotep, stated, "If you are in a position of one to whom petitions are made, be courteous and listen to the petitioner's story. Do not stop his words until he has poured out all that is in his heart and has said all that he came to say. A man with a grievance loves the official who will accept what he states and let him talk out his trouble fully. . . ." No better advice can be given today.

• A foundry foreman settled a grievance by following this basic principle. A very angry employee complained vehemently to this foreman that he had been unjustly assigned to do a job which he considered to be especially undesirable. The job called for heavy physical effort and it was a hot and dirty one. The foreman listened patiently and sympathetically to the employee's tirade until he stopped, but said nothing, just waited attentively. The employee repeated his grievance, but in a much calmer manner. When he stopped talking this time, the foreman asked, "If you were in my place, how would you settle this grievance?" The employee hesitated briefly, then replied, "I guess I don't really have a grievance after all. Other guys have had to do this same job before me. I feel better now that I've shot off my mouth."

This story points up the importance of listening patiently and with an open-minded attitude. It was not only how long the foreman listened, but how well, that produced the desired result. Frequently an employee given the opportunity to vocalize his grievance to an understanding boss two or three times realizes that it was not as important as he first thought. But the foreman must have a sincere interest in the employee's problem. Any lack of sincerity will be noticed by the employee, and he will then be convinced that his grievance will not get fair consideration. It is sometimes difficult for a foreman who thinks a grievance is trivial to show a deep and sincere interest in it, but he should keep in mind that it is not trivial to the employee.

Important Points

1. It is essential that the supervisor listen attentively, without interrupting, and with sincere interest in order to determine the grievant's point of view.

2. He should encourage the grievant to talk, ask him leading questions, and get him to repeat his grievance if he is still excited.

• Sometimes a supervisor must look beyond an aggrieved employee's voiced grievance to detect the real cause. A case of this kind happened in an aircraft instrument assembly department. During a period of six weeks, several assemblers submitted grievances involving working conditions, wages, and assignment of overtime. The morale in this department had previously been good; formal grievances had seldom occurred.

The personnel director, who was involved in the second step of the grievance procedure, suspected that these grievances were symptoms of a deeper problem, since he was able to resolve them amicably whereas the foreman had been unable to settle any of them in the first step.

This foreman had been appointed about five months earlier when the previous foreman was transferred to a different plant. The new foreman was a young man who had been an assistant foreman in a different department for less than a year before he was promoted to be foreman of the assembly department. He was a technical school graduate and was well qualified so far as job knowledge was concerned.

The personnel director finally was able to get two of the grievants to express their true feelings, which proved that his hunch about a deeper problem was correct. There were two basic sources of dissatisfaction which caused the grievances. First, the employees resented the appointment of an outsider from a different department instead of one of their own group. Second, the new foreman had used his authority in a rather heavy-handed manner. The result was that the employees disliked their new boss, although they respected him for his knowledge and technical skill.

The personnel director had a heart-to-heart talk with the foreman, who admitted that he might have misused his authority in his desire to make a good production record. Fortunately, this young man learned from his mistakes. He called his employees together, admitted that he had abused his authority, recognized that he had fumbled the handling of their grievances, and conveyed the impression that he really was not so tough. He made a sincere effort by his subsequent actions to gain their confidence as well as their respect, and eventually he succeeded.

Important Point

Sometimes a grievant does not state the true, underlying cause of his grievance, especially if it really stems from resentment against the supervisor. It is important, however, to discover the true cause so it can be resolved.

Putting the Grievant at Ease

When an employee presents a complaint, either informally or as a formal grievance, the supervisor's first step should be to put the employee at ease. He should realize that most employees are nervous, tense, emotionally upset, and possibly a bit fearful when they initiate a grievance. The employee needs to be reassured that his supervisor is willing to discuss his problem calmly, objectively, and sympathetically. It is important that the supervisor maintain a friendly attitude, without a chip on his shoulder. His attitude should convey to the employee, "You have every right to talk to me about anything connected with your job or your relationship with me which displeases you. I want to understand your point of view. I'm glad you came to me with this problem so I can have a chance to correct it." If the supervisor is sincere, such a beginning will probably put the employee at ease. Then he should give the employee all the time he needs to unburden himself. The supervisor must be a good listener. When the employee realizes that the supervisor does not resent his presenting the grievance, he will relax. The supervisor must guard against becoming excited even though the grievant or his spokesman may be. A kind word at the right time will have a reassuring effect.

Once the grievant or his spokesman has started to talk about his grievance, the supervisor should be patient and not interrupt him. After he has talked himself out, the supervisor can ask questions to clarify any doubtful points or misstatements. The supervisor must show his readiness to give openminded consideration to what the aggrieved employee or his steward has to say.

Important Points

1. The supervisor should attempt to make the grievant feel at ease in presenting his grievance.
2. He should indicate that he does not resent the employee's having a grievance, but rather that he is anxious to eliminate any source of irritation.

Discussing the Grievance

The grievance should be dealt with by discussion; the supervisor must avoid letting it deteriorate into an argument. No one really wins an argument. Each party to an argument becomes more fixed in the belief that he is right and the other is wrong. Arguments become inflamed by emotions. Each party becomes more interested in winning the argument than in reaching a fair solution to the problem. The supervisor who lets himself be drawn into an argument generally loses his dignity, poise, and self-respect, and may be inclined to consider the grievance as a personal affront rather than a problem which must be considered on a factual basis. Calm discussion, on the other hand, permits the supervisor to settle the grievance by reasonable evaluation of the facts without resort to antagonism or a show of authority. Such a settlement is more likely to be mutually satisfactory and lasting.

Important Point

A supervisor should not permit a grievance discussion to deteriorate into a heated argument, for nothing can be accomplished if this occurs. Calm discussion of the facts without show of authority is generally more likely to produce a fair solution of the problem.

Getting the Facts

A supervisor cannot possibly resolve a grievance fairly unless he first gets the story straight. He must get the grievant's story from beginning to end. It must be clear and complete. Having heard the employee's grievance once, the supervisor should, by a series of questions, get him to repeat it a second time, and even a third time, at least the most important parts of the grievance. The point is that the grievant should be encouraged to repeat the grievance until his emotional temperature has subsided to normal. Each time he gets it off his chest the grievance tends to assume more reasonable proportions in his own mind. Any discrepancies are more likely to show up each time the grievance is related. The supervisor is then better able to distinguish between facts and opinions. Having obtained a complete and accurate description of the problem from the grievant's viewpoint, the supervisor is in a better position to deal justly with the grievance.

In many cases, the supervisor must investigate further to obtain all the facts. Unless he gets all the facts, he may become the victim of a misunderstanding. In one case, the employee complained to the foreman that he had not received all the overtime pay to which he was entitled. The foreman was inclined to believe that the employee was right, but fortunately did not say so to the employee. He checked with the payroll department and got complete records to show that the employee had been properly compensated for all his regular and overtime pay for the last six months. When confronted with these records the employee could see for himself that he had no grievance.

The supervisor should consult with all other persons whose knowledge of the situation can contribute to an understanding of the problem. If the grievant is aware that what he says may be checked with others having knowledge of the problem, he is likely to avoid inaccurate statements. But the supervisor must avoid an attitude of suspicion or disbelief; rather he should tactfully give the impression that he is searching for facts which will help him to arrive at a fair decision.

Important Points

A supervisor should get all the facts he can to help him arrive at a fair decision about a grievance. He should proceed
1. By encouraging grievant to repeat his side of the story to be sure that he understands the employee's viewpoint, and so that the employee becomes more calm;
2. By consulting with others who may be able to contribute pertinent information;
3. By evaluating facts and opinions given to him;
4. By checking any pertinent records which may be available.

Considering the Grievant's Viewpoint

The importance of considering the employee's point of view has already been mentioned. This is necessary before the supervisor can know what action to take. He must not assume that the employee or the steward is wrong; he may be right. If the employee's viewpoint is completely wrong, the supervisor will, of course, have to give him an unwelcome answer. But it is especially important in such a case for the supervisor to give his decision in the best way to get acceptance by the employee. The employee may not accept an unfavorable decision, but the supervisor should try to avoid irritating him further. On the other hand, if the supervisor gives his unfavorable decision objectively, backed by logical reasons, sometimes the employee will accept it as a fair decision which overrides his objections, especially if he realizes that the supervisor has thoroughly understood his point of view and has given it honest consideration.

Important Point

An employee will accept an adverse decision about his grievance only if he believes the supervisor has a good understanding of his point of view, and has given it proper consideration.

Avoiding Snap Judgments

Most supervisors will find difficulty in maintaining an unprejudiced attitude when employees come to them with grievances. The supervisor's first reaction is likely to be one of defensiveness—the feeling that the employee is threatening his authority as boss. But he should push this feeling into the background; otherwise his emotional reaction may force him into making a snap judgment before he has obtained all the facts. If this happens, he may give the grievant the impression that he has already made up his mind, that he has prejudged the case.

• A snap decision which boomeranged for this reason involved a grievance about a piecework rate. An employee complained to his foreman that he could not make out on the newly established piecework rate. The foreman replied arrogantly, "That rate was set by careful time study and I'm sure it is right. I don't think you have given it a good try so I won't do anything about it." The shop steward was not satisfied, knowing that the employee was a competent man, not a chronic complainer. He and the employee took the grievance to the second step. The rate was rechecked. An arithmetical error in computing the rate was uncovered and corrected. This put the foreman in a very embarrassing position.

If a supervisor is irritated when a grievance is presented, and most supervisors are on occasion, he must steel himself to remain calm, be patient, hear the grievance to the end, search for the facts, and postpone making a decision. He should tell the employee and the shop steward he needs a little time to consider the grievance and to investigate the facts. (Of course, he must arrive at a decision promptly within the time allotted by the grievance procedure.) Even if his original snap judgment turns out to be correct, he will have the satisfaction of knowing that he analyzed the problem correctly and based his final decision on facts rather than on a hunch. Also, there is always the danger that a snap judgment, especially if favorable to the grievant, may turn out to be a boomerang.

A snap decision may set a precedent which will cause trouble in the future, or it might be unfair to other employees. Action which seems expedient at the moment should not be taken if it is basically unsound, and therefore likely to cause other problems. If a snap decision, though correct, is unfavorable to the grievant, he will probably feel that his grievance did not receive fair consideration.

It is especially tempting for the supervisor to jump to a conclusion when the grievance appears to lack merit or is obviously imaginary. But he must remember that the aggrieved employee believes his grievance is justified, and it must be dealt with as if it were. The supervisor who makes the mistake of deciding a grievance by jumping to a conclusion will undermine his reputation for fair dealing.

Important Points

1. The supervisor must avoid making snap decisions. He should never make a decision about a grievance before he has obtained all the facts he can get.

2. Snap judgments are frequently prompted by anger or prejudice; such decisions are usually wrong.

Evaluating Facts and Opinions

No decision about a grievance should be reached before all pertinent facts and opinions have been obtained and evaluated by the supervisor. First of all, he must distinguish between the two. A fact is something which actually exists, something true which cannot be denied. An opinion is a conclusion which may be questioned.

• An office supervisor was continually harassed by complaints from the women about the temperature of their air-conditioned office. Some complained they were freezing, others said the office was too warm. Some wanted to open windows near them to relieve the stuffy atmosphere in the room. The supervisor arranged for the maintenance department to try different settings of the thermostat, but no setting was satisfactory. Finally she called the women together, explained that the windows must be kept closed when the air-conditioner was operating to eliminate excessive humidity, and asked each one what actual temperature she would prefer. Their replies varied from 68° F. to 73° F. The supervisor finally got them to agree that 70° F. would be acceptable, pointing out that those who wanted a higher temperature would find 70° F. comfortable with a sweater or a jacket over their shoulders, and that those who wanted it cooler could wear lighter clothes. A few of the women who liked higher temperatures were moved away from the air-conditioning outlets, and those who wanted a cooler temperature were put under the outlets where there was a slight draft. The supervisor had several thermometers installed in various locations in the office. After a couple of weeks there were no more complaints about temperature. At first, the supervisor noticed that occasionally a woman would leave her desk to read the nearest thermometer, and then go back to work. The thermometer reading of 70° F. was a fact which overrode the women's opinions about the rooms being too cold or too warm.

If a worker complains that he has not been given his fair share of overtime work, this is an opinion. If the foreman replies that he has had his fair share, this can also be only an opinion. But if the foreman shows the employee time records proving that the employee has averaged 3.1 hours overtime per week as compared to the department's average of 2.9 hours per week, this is a fact which the employee will accept.

Opinions, though not as important as facts, should be given proper consideration and weight. In some cases it will be necessary to give considerable weight to opinions because it is impossible to obtain enough facts which have a bearing on the grievance.

When the factual evidence is inadequate to give a clear-cut answer to the problem, the supervisor should give the employee the benefit of the doubt. Squabbling over petty details encourages an uncompromising attitude on the part of the other person, while giving in on an unimportant point may help to soften the other person's hard feelings.

Most important, if a supervisor discovers he has made a mistake, he should admit it. Frankly admitting an error will not injure his prestige, but attempting to cover up a mistake or stubbornly refusing to admit it will cast doubt on his integrity. The following example illustrates this point.

• A shipping clerk processed a rush shipment of machine repair parts by air freight in accordance with verbal instructions from his supervisor. The customer reported that one of the essential parts they had received was not what they had ordered. Although the shipping supervisor then realized that he had given an incorrect part number to the clerk, he tried to cover up his own mistake by insisting that it was the clerk's error, and imposed a three-day disciplinary suspension on the clerk. The shipping clerk filed a grievance. His shop steward investigated the grievance and discovered that another employee had overheard the instructions given by the supervisor and verified the clerk's contention that he had shipped the part he was told to ship. When the steward confronted the supervisor with this information, he backed down and grudgingly admitted he might have been in error.

Willingness on the part of a supervisor to admit a mistake encourages the grievant and his steward to admit any mistake they might have made. Refusal to admit a mistake, especially if it is obvious, may embitter the aggrieved employee and his spokesman, causing them to become unreasonable.

Making the Decision

After obtaining and evaluating all facts and opinions objectively, and weighing possible consequences of the decision, the supervisor must make his decision promptly within the time limit specified by the grievance procedure. He should strive for the most logical and equitable decision.

• It is not always easy to determine what is logical and equitable. In one situation, a supervisor had a day shift and a night shift. For some time past he had assigned married men to the day shift and single men to the night shift. He thought this was logical because he felt that married men should spend their evenings at home with their families. But he began to get complaints from some of the single men. Some of them complained that they could not have a normal social life unless they had some evenings for dating, parties, theater, and so forth. The foreman was finally convinced that this was a valid complaint.

He discovered that relatively few men liked permanent assignment to the night shift, even though they received a 10-percent shift bonus. When he polled the night shift to determine which, if any, preferred this shift, only two did. One young man was a part-time student who attended day classes; the other man wanted the extra money provided by the shift differential. The rest of the men on both shifts, whether married or single, agreed that it would be fair to alternate them on the two shifts every four weeks. What the foreman considered logical turned out not to be completely so as far as his employees were concerned.

The aggrieved employee and his steward must be satisfied that the supervisor's decision about a grievance is equitable. If either of them thinks the decision was biased it will be unacceptable. A supervisor is sometimes inclined to be prejudiced when an employee presents a grievance, but he must avoid letting his prejudice influence his decision. When he has reached a decision, he should ask himself, "Is this a decision I would accept if I were the grievant and he were my boss?" He should further ask himself, "If the grievant were my favorite employee, would I have made the same decision?" If he can honestly answer yes to both these questions, he has probably made an objective decision. If he cannot, he should reconsider his decision before giving the grievant the answer.

Important Points

1. A supervisor should strive for the most logical and most equitable decision, but he should try to understand what the grievant would consider to be logical; it may not be the same as his own opinion.
2. He must not let prejudice influence his decision.

Appropriate Discipline

It is important that the disciplinary action taken by the company be appropriate to the offense. In the past, discharge was frequently the only penalty, irrespective of the offense. Lesser penalties, such as a written warning or suspension for a period of time, were infrequent.

Today, except for major offenses, an employee will first be given a warning. If he repeats the offense, he will probably be given a disciplinary suspension, which will vary according to the nature of the offense, and he will usually be discharged for the third offense.

This pattern is the result of arbitration awards. Arbitrators will not sustain the discharge of a longtime employee for a first offense unless it is a serious one, such as theft. The discharge of an employee with many years of seniority is often called "capital punishment" because the discharged employee also loses his job security. On his new job he will be at the bottom of the seniority list and will be one of the first to be laid off.

Arbitrators feel that a worker should be warned and then disciplined before he is discharged for offenses other than the most serious ones. Seniority is given a great deal of weight in their determination of the appropriate penalty.

The supervisor will be in a much better position to win his arbitration case if he observes the following rules in imposing discipline:

1. Distinguish between serious and minor offenses.
2. Distinguish between long-service employees and those recently employed.
3. Except when a major offense has been committed, give the employee a written warning and a disciplinary suspension before discharging him.
4. Vary the penalty according to the nature of the offense.
5. Impose similar penalties for similar offenses involving different employees. Be consistent.

Communicating the Decision

The manner in which a decision about a grievance is handed down may be important as far as its acceptance by the grievant is concerned. Too quick a decision, even when favorable to the grievant, may indicate that the supervisor knew all along that he was wrong and the grievant was right. If the decision is unfavorable and too quickly conveyed, the grievant may feel that the supervisor's mind was set against him from the beginning. Hence timing within the specified time limit is important. Both the one who makes the decision and the one who receives it must be satisfied that the decision is honest, equitable, and arrived at objectively.

In the case of certain grievances, such as those involving company rules or policy, the supervisor may be tempted to pass the buck. He must not imply that he does not agree with the policy or rule involved, but rather should explain the reasons behind the policy and try to convince the grievant that it is fair and proper. He should never say to the employee, "I'd like to decide in your favor but I haven't the authority." If he does not have the authority to settle the grievance, he should frankly tell the grievant so, and add that he will get a decision from his superior who does have the authority.

If the decision is unfavorable to the grievant, the supervisor cannot dodge the issue—he will have to give a negative answer. He must not try to "straddle," but should give his unfavorable answer straightforwardly, calmly, and considerately. He should give full reasons for his answer in a patient, sympathetic, and gently persuasive manner, trying to convey that if the grievance were justified and could be granted, he would be pleased to give an affirmative answer.

There is another thing which the supervisor should do, if possible, when a decision is unfavorable: He should try to help the grievant and the steward to save face. Nobody likes to be proved wrong. The worst thing a supervisor can do at such a time is to gloat over his success in winning the battle with the grievant. He should never rub it in. Instead, the supervisor will gain in stature if he can honestly say to the grievant, "I can understand why you felt as you did, since you had only part of the facts," or "I hope now you realize that your grievance was due to a misunderstanding." The important thing is that the supervisor convey to the grievant and the steward that he does not resent their presenting the grievance, that he is glad he had the opportunity to clarify and resolve a troublesome situation, and that he looks forward to their cooperation in the future.

Important Points

1. A grievance decision must be given to the grievant within the specified time limit and in the proper manner.

2. If the decision is unfavorable to the employee, the supervisor must make an unwelcome but definite statement, calmly and without smugness.

3. If possible, he should try to "save face" for the grievant.

4. If favorable to the employee, the decision should be given without resentment.

GUIDING PRINCIPLES FOR SHOP STEWARDS

A shop steward must know his local union contract thoroughly, especially the grievance procedure, in order to represent the members. But there is more he should know. Like the supervisor, he should find the following basic principles effective:

1. Listen to the grievant's complaint carefully and patiently. Be alert to detect the true cause.

2. Put the employee at ease. Help him to maintain composure.

3. Get the story straight. Get all the facts. Ask questions to clarify any doubtful points. Distinguish between facts and opinions.

4. Avoid snap judgment. Investigate the grievance. Talk to others who may be able to supply pertinent information. Refer to any records which can supply facts.

5. Evaluate all facts and opinions before deciding what action should be taken. If the grievance is not justified, tell the employee so and explain why.

6. Process the grievance promptly and vigorously if it is justified, but be fair and accurate in presenting the

facts. Do not exaggerate. Avoid threats, name-calling, and anger. Don't rub it in if you win the case.

7. Take the grievance to the next step if you do not get a satisfactory settlement, or confer with other union officials regarding the next move to be taken.

8. Keep complete and accurate records of the grievance negotiations. Keep the local union officers informed at all times.

Listening to the Employee's Complaint

A shop steward should listen patiently and carefully to an employee's problem, just as a supervisor should. The steward will probably have less trouble detecting the true cause of the grievance than the supervisor, especially if the grievance stems from resentment about something the supervisor did or failed to do. An employee usually does not hesitate to tell his steward when he is disgruntled about his supervisor's actions. In fact, the employee may exaggerate. The steward may have to get him calmed down before his statement of the grievance gives the true picture.

Important Points

1. A shop steward should listen carefully to an employee's complaint, and must be sure he understands the employee's viewpoint.

2. He should try to determine whether he is learning the true cause of the grievance.

Putting the Employee at Ease

The steward can help to put the grievant at ease by calming him, helping him to dissipate his anger, restoring his self-confidence if necessary, and in other ways helping him to maintain composure during grievance processing. Generally, it is best for the steward to serve as spokesman, thus relieving the grievant of tension and emotional upset. If the shop steward is the spokesman, he can guide and control the presentation of the grievance, and can call on the employee to provide only factual statements which will strengthen his case without getting him into a battle of wits with the supervisor. The steward should determine how much participation in the negotiations the grievant is able to take without losing his composure. Some employees are not very articulate, but those that are should be given the opportunity to present their own case, although the steward should remain the spokesman. The steward should always try to control the presentation, and should ask for a recess if the employee loses his composure.

Important Points

1. The steward should try to calm any grievant who is angry, and should put at ease a nervous or timid employee.

2. The steward should be the spokesman, especially if the employee is not very articulate or if he is tense and apprehensive.

Getting the Story Straight

It is important that the shop steward get complete and accurate information before he processes a grievance. He must get all the facts in order to present the grievances effectively. He must listen to the aggrieved employee's story from beginning to end, and should ask questions to clarify any doubtful points. He should analyze what the employee has told him to determine what are facts and what are opinions. He may have to have the employee repeat his story in order to get it straight.

Important Point

It is important for a steward to get the whole story from the employee before he can process a grievance effectively.

Avoiding Snap Judgments

Like the supervisor, the shop steward must guard against making snap judgments, and he must also be sure before the grievance is presented that it is based on sound premises. He must be especially careful to avoid snap judgments if the supervisor happens to be unpopular.

The steward should investigate the alleged grievance by talking with other employees who may have information which has a bearing on it. He should further investigate by checking production records, time records, previous grievance settlements, or any other sources which will help to evaluate the current situation or to differentiate between fact and opinion. The steward must be in a position to present facts which support his claims; his case will be weakened if the supervisor can prove that he has made any misstatements.

Important Points

1. A steward must guard against making snap decisions, just as a supervisor must.
2. He must consider all the facts before deciding whether a grievance is justified.
3. He, too, must avoid letting bias influence his decision.

Evaluating Facts and Opinions

A shop steward must evaluate all the facts and opinions he has obtained before he can reach the proper decision about a grievance.

If the steward's analysis convinces him that the employee does not have a justified grievance, he should tell the employee so, giving the reasons why he thinks so. It is unwise to submit a grievance which obviously cannot be won. If there is doubt, however, the grievance should be processed. It may be wise for the steward to discuss the problem with the chief steward or other officer of his local before deciding that a grievance has no merit. If he believes that the grievance is justified, he should submit it promptly and process it vigorously but without hostility.

Important Point

All facts and opinions must be carefully evaluated by the steward in order to determine whether the grievance is valid, and to develop the most effective presentation if a decision is made to process it.

Presenting the Grievance—First Step

It is important for the steward to abide by the established grievance procedure in every respect. Most union contracts require that a shop steward check with his foreman before he leaves his job to investigate a grievance; this rule should be followed carefully, as should all other requirements for presenting the grievance.

The steward should plan his approach by deciding the most important points and how he will present them to the supervisor. He should have available any records which will help him to prove his statements. It is wise for him to bring written notes to jog his memory if he should forget any point he plans to make.

In nearly all cases, the steward should act as principal spokesman in presenting a grievance. He is better informed about the procedure, is usually more articulate than the employee, and is not so likely to become emotionally upset, so can control the discussion more effectively. He should not let the discussion get sidetracked into irrelevant channels, but should insist that the foreman stick to the specific issue involved in the grievance.

The steward should present his facts forcefully but not militantly. He must be accurate and should not exaggerate. He should avoid any threats, insults, or unreasonable statements, and should control his temper even if the supervisor becomes abusive. The steward has a right to expect decent treatment from the supervisor, and if he does not get it, he should not hesitate to talk back, but name-calling, open anger, insults, and the like should be avoided; these are evidence that one lacks self-confidence or feels insecure. It is best to be calm, straight-foward, even friendly, but firm and self-assured as well.

The steward should never get into an argument with the grievant or another union representative in the presence of the foreman or other company official. He can always ask for a brief recess from the grievance discussion when necessary to settle a disagreement or misunderstanding with the employee.

The steward should do his best to get the grievance settled in the first step. He should keep in mind that management dislikes reversing a supervisor's first-step decision, and therefore will usually try hard in later steps of the procedure to justify the first-step decision. If the steward is successful in getting a favorable decision in the first step, he should not rub it in. It is wise for the steward to remain on good terms with the supervisor; it might even be desirable for him to tell the supervisor that he appreciates his honesty and sincerity. This could make the next grievance proceedings easier for the steward.

If the grievance procedure requires that the grievance be put in writing in the first step, the grievant, supervisor, and steward should all sign the written grievance, and each should be given a copy. Even if the procedure does not call for a written grievance in step one, it may be desirable for the steward to put the decision in writing. This will prevent any misunderstanding from developing later.

If the first-step decision is unsatisfactory, the steward should tell the supervisor so, and let him know that the grievance will be referred to the second step.

Processing the Grievance—Step Two

Practically all formal grievance procedures require that the grievance be put in writing at the second step, if not at the first. It is the shop steward's responsibility to make sure that the grievance is properly put in writing, usually on a form provided for this purpose.

If a satisfactory agreement cannot be reached in the first step, the steward should initiate the appeal to process the second step of the grievance in accordance with the established procedure. He should confer with the proper officials of the local and get their approval to go to the second step. Usually this ends the steward's direct participation in the procedure, but he may be brought into union strategy discussion to provide information and to assist in any way he can. In any case, he should keep in close touch with the subsequent proceedings, and should keep the aggrieved employee informed about the progress of his case.

Maintaining Grievance Records

Reference has already been made to the need for adequate records, but the importance of this should be stressed. The steward should write a brief report of every action he takes as soon as possible after taking it. His records should start with the statements made by the employee when he first presents his complaint to the steward. Each written record should be dated and all pertinent information should be included.

Although a large majority of grievances are settled in the first step, some may have to go to arbitration for settlement. If this happens, complete and accurate records will be helpful in the arbitration process. Documentation of arbitration cases will be further discussed in Chapter 7.

From the beginning of a grievance and throughout the grievance proceedings, the steward should keep his union officials completely informed. He should discuss the case with them frequently, and should seek their advice whenever he has any doubt about how to proceed. Every grievance, no matter how small, is an important part of the union's business about which the union office should be kept fully informed.

Important Points

1. Complete written records should be kept by shop stewards on each grievance processed.

2. Records should include all important information in considerable detail so it will be available in case the grievance is not settled in the first step or prior to arbitration.

3. Records are especially important if a grievance should go finally to arbitration.

5 | Grievance Procedures

INTRODUCTION

One of the most significant developments in labor-management relations during the past 25 years has been the development of procedures for handling employee complaints. It has become recognized that there is a need for the orderly processing of employee grievances. In the absence of such procedures, employee frustration and dissatisfaction can result in lower production and higher turnover. Although employee complaints are sometimes unjustified, or stem from misunderstandings, a great many grievances are justified. If there is no procedure for objectively considering and settling these complaints, industrial unrest will inevitably result.

    • In one case the men noticed that one man in the department was receiving more overtime work from the supervisor than the others. When it was learned that this man was the son-in-law of the general foreman they came to the conclusion that the supervisor was trying to get in good with his boss. Without a grievance procedure to correct the situation, antagonisms would soon have disrupted the work in the department.

    • In another situation a foreman was assigned to supervise the work of a department which previously had had no supervisor. The men resented the assignment of someone to supervise them. Their resentment turned into open hostility when the new supervisor, a fellow worker, exercised his authority with a heavy hand and issued orders in an autocratic manner. When he suspended a man for talking back, a grievance was filed. Since this was the first disciplinary measure taken by the supervisor, the company felt that if it did not back him up he would be unable to perform his work.

At the arbitration hearing it became obvious to all present that both the men and the supervisor used poor judgment. As a result of the arbitration hearing there was a decided improvement in the working relationship between the men and the foreman.

• Another company was faced with the problem of frequent walkouts by its employees, instigated by the shop steward, who called the men off the job whenever he disagreed with management. If he thought that a management decision violated the contract he would notify all the men to stop work. The company finally discharged the shop steward, and the discharge was upheld. The arbitrator held that the union violated the contract by stopping work instead of filing a grievance and processing it through the grievance-arbitration machinery. After this award all work stoppages ceased.

Almost all union grievance procedures terminate in arbitration, a private judicial system for settling disputes arising between employees and employers. It is the counterpart of our system of courts and judges who settle civil disputes.

The mere existence of a grievance-arbitration procedure tends to prevent arbitrary acts. If a man knows that his decisions are subject to review by a grievance committee and ultimately by an arbitrator, he is likely to be more careful in his judgments and decisions. A supervisor will think before he acts because he knows that his decision may be challenged.

Important Point

The existence of a grievance-arbitration procedure tends to forestall arbitrary acts by both management and the union.

Pitfalls of Decision Making

• A supervisor who was not favorably disposed toward the shop steward saw him talking to an employee and suspended him for three days for neglecting his work. At the hearing the supervisor had to admit that, even though he could not hear what the men were talking about, he had assumed that it was idle talk. Yet the employee and the shop steward testified that their conversation related to a pending grievance which was legitimate union business.

• An employee in a cafeteria was discharged for not depositing money he collected from a customer in the cash register. The customer was in fact an employee of an agency checking on the honesty of the employee, and when he noticed that the employee held the money in his hand and failed to ring it up on the cash register, he reported him immediately to the manager, who promptly discharged the employee. At the arbitration hearing it was brought out that the employee had written a note on a napkin and had attempted to give it to the manager, who refused to accept it. The note, which was submitted to the arbitrator, stated: "I think this customer is a detective. He has not paid the sales tax; what should I do with his money?" Moreover, the employee tried to explain why he had not deposited the money in the cash register but the manager refused to listen.

These incidents show that all people, including supervisors, can make false assumptions and come to false conclusions. It is important to have a system which can correct these errors.

By having grievance-arbitration procedures, a company can improve the morale and efficiency of its employees as well as their job satisfaction. Other results will be a decline in turnover, absenteeism, tardiness, and other symptoms of employee dissatisfaction.

Important Point

In making decisions, supervisors should avoid pitfalls such as making false assumptions and failing to get all the facts.

Handling Employee Complaints in a Nonunion Company

Whenever large groups of people work under supervision, whether they are unionized or not, employee complaints are inevitable. It is normal for people to have differences of opinion. No one, whether employee or supervisor, is always fair and reasonable.

In most nonunionized companies it is very difficult to appeal a supervisor's decision. As a result dissatisfied employees must either live with their frustrations or quit. Moreover, if a supervisor knows that his decisions cannot be challenged, he will frequently make them without thinking them through. Merely because employees' complaints are not vocal does not mean that they do not exist.

In recognition of this problem, many nonunionized companies have established appeals procedures. They have found, however, that in order for these systems to function properly, supervisors must be given intensive training in how to make objective decisions. Most people are unaware of the mental process by which people and situations are evaluated. The decision-making process will be discussed in Chapter 6.

Important Points

1. Grievance procedures are becoming fairly common in nonunionized companies. Management is beginning to realize that there is a need to appeal supervisors' decisions which employees consider unjust.

2. Supervisors are likely to make more equitable decisions if the employees can appeal.

Grievance Procedure in a Nonunionized Bank

The following appeals system, established by a large metropolitan bank, is an illustration of a grievance procedure in a nonunionized company. (It should be noted that there is no provision for final and binding arbitration). A facsimile of the grievance-procedure chart appears on pages 106–107.

is something about your job worrying you?
Tell us about it . . .
CONFIDENTIALLY

CHANNEL FOR EMPLOYEE RELATIONS PROCEDURE

Step 1
SUPERVISING OFFICER

↓

Step 2
OFFICER IN CHARGE

↓

Step 3
AREA SUPERVISOR

↓

Step 4
PERSONNEL POLICY COMMITTEE

ALTERNATE CHANNELS

When a problem personally involves an officer who functions at any step in the procedure, you may omit that step and proceed to the next one.

You may write directly to the Personnel Policy Committee if the matter is of such a nature that you do not wish to discuss it orally at any step.

You may consult officers and counselors of the personnel department at any time if the subject is of a personal or embarrassing nature, or if advice on use of the procedure is desired.

If you indicate that you wish your name to remain undisclosed, it will not be divulged without your permission.

— fill out this form, submit as follows: —

EMPLOYEE RELATIONS PROCEDURE

NAME _____ DATE _____
(Please print)

BRANCH OR
HOME ADDRESS _____ DEPARTMENT _____

_____

STATEMENT OF PROBLEM

_____

_____

_____

_____

_____

_____

_____

_____

_____

_____

_____

_____

_____

_____

_____
Signature

AVAILING YOURSELF OF THIS PROCEDURE WILL IN NO
WAY ADVERSELY AFFECT YOUR STANDING IN THE BANK,
YOUR OPPORTUNITY FOR ADVANCEMENT OR YOUR
SALARY PROGRESS.

Under this system, known as the "Employee Relations Procedure," the following instructions are issued to all supervisors regarding the manner in which they are to handle grievances:

"The success of the Employee Relations Procedure rests largely with you—the officers and supervisors who administer it and who conduct interviews at the various steps involved.

"The bank views the procedure as an important avenue for the expression of employee attitudes on working conditions and personnel relationships in general. The bank expects that an employee utilizing this procedure will be given a sympathetic and understanding hearing, and that where corrective action is indicated such action will be taken consistent with bank policy and good personnel practice.

"The Employee Relations Procedure is open to any employee who believes that the treatment he or she receives on the job is inequitable or unfair, or for any other reason needs correction. This applies to all phases of an employee's relations with the bank, including subjects of pay, promotion, job operations, discipline, conduct of fellow workers, and supervision.

"Lacking an opportunity to adjust such complaints, an employee may become a dissatisfied employee. His dissatisfaction may be reflected in the performance of his job and adversely affect our high standard of customer service. Therefore, good employee relations is good business.

"To avoid the development of a situation into a problem, be on the alert for circumstances or for working conditions which may become the subject of employee dissatisfaction. Voluntarily correct them as promptly as possible. If you do this, you will not only gain the esteem of your staff because of your own interest, but you will also keep minor problems from becoming major ones. It holds true that 'an ounce of prevention is worth a pound of cure.'

"It is important that our employees have full confidence in the workings of the procedure itself as well as in the prompt and effective handling of problems by their supervisors. It is fundamental that no employee should believe that he or she will be discriminated against in any way because this procedure is utilized to discuss a problem. The "proof of the pudding" in this respect will be the way in which the program is operated, and the spirit in which you as supervisors follow through in the important role you play in all phases of the Procedure.

"To assist you in carrying out your supervisory responsibilities, some suggestions are set forth in this pamphlet. (It is also suggested that you familiarize yourselves with the booklet entitled *Employee Relations Procedure* that has been distributed to all employees.)

"1. *Put the employee at ease.*

At the start of a discussion, put the employee at ease by friendly remarks. When he comes to you with his problem he may be upset, perhaps embarrassed. Be relaxed and make it apparent that you are. Allow the employee sufficient time to get accustomed to the interview and to gain confidence both in himself and in you. Convey to him that he can freely exchange ideas and opinions with you. Make certain that he realizes you are giving his problem an objective hearing.

"2. *Listen patiently to the employee's problem.*

Employees using this procedure do so for a reason, and it is important to them. Therefore, be a patient listener and encourage a full discussion. Ask questions only to secure pertinent facts.

"3. *Do not argue.*

Be objective and unbiased. Do not get emotionally involved. Never argue with the employee about conflicting points of view and never reprimand an employee during the discussion of his problem. This would be contrary to the purpose and intent of the program.

"4. *Investigate the problem thoroughly.*

Get all the facts and investigate each problem thoroughly. Do not make snap decisions. Never make a decision until all the facts are before you. Consider the problem from all viewpoints.

"5. *Take action promptly.*

If the employee's problem requires some action on your part for solution, such as taking the matter up with your superior or with a staff department that might be concerned, take this action promptly. Do not put it off. When the problem is such that an immediate decision cannot be made, assure the employee that you will give it your prompt consideration. Inform the employee of your decision as soon as it has been made and discuss the reasons with him.

"6. *Explain the employee relations procedure to the employee.*

If you are unable to satisfy the employee at your step in the procedure, let him know that he may avail himself of the opportunity for review by the officer next in the line of procedure, and assure him that his discussion with you and any subsequent appeal will in no way adversely affect his standing in the bank, his opportunity for advancement, or his salary progress. It is your responsibility throughout your discussions with the employee to make it clear that he is getting an unbiased, sincere, and sympathetic hearing. The successful operation of the plan depends upon the impression you create. Should an employee request that his discussion with you remain confidential, make sure that his wishes in this regard are respected. If, however, the problem is of such a nature that it cannot be settled without revealing the employee's identity, explain to him why this is necessary.

"Four steps have been provided in the procedure. It is expected that most problems will be settled in the early steps, and this is desirable. However, it should be made clear to the employee that he is free to use later steps if he wishes to do so.

"While emphasis has been placed upon the use of this procedure by employees below the rank of supervising officer, the bank desires that all personnel, including officers, be afforded the opportunities for discussion provided by the procedure. Officer morale and well-being are of vital concern to management. Therefore, any officer who wishes to do so may use this procedure. Officers are given the same firm assurance provided all other employees: Use of the procedure will in no way adversely affect his standing in the bank, his opportunities for advancement, or his salary progress.

"The bank urges the full cooperation of all officers and all supervisors in carrying out both the spirit and the intent of the Employee Relations Procedure."

Union Grievance Procedures

Over 95 percent of all collective bargaining agreements contain a grievance procedure terminating in final and binding arbitration.

Some of these procedures are simple, others very detailed. It is important that the shop steward and the supervisor become thoroughly familiar with the procedure they must follow. Both must be particularly careful to observe the time limits specified.

The following is a typical grievance procedure terminating in arbitration, taken from a collective bargaining contract:

Settlement of Disputes and Arbitration

(a) The union may designate two (2) chief shop stewards and one (1) assistant chief shop steward within its jurisdiction. It shall be the function of such stewards to assist in the adjustment of all grievances in accordance with the grievance procedure set forth below. For a grievance to be recognized by the company, it must be submitted within seven (7) calendar days following the alleged act, except that where employee time cards are involved in a grievance, the union shall have seven (7) days after the time cards are made available. The following is the grievance procedure:

Step 1. The aggrieved employee and his shop steward shall meet and discuss the grievance with the foreman. If not satisfactorily adjusted in three (3) working days, then the grievance shall be reduced to writing and Step 2 should be taken.

The above step does not prohibit or preclude filing of a grievance by the grievance committee where the union considers it necessary. In such cases the grievance committee shall specify the employee or employees alleged to have been aggrieved.

Step 2. The shop steward shall meet with the department head for discussion of the grievance. If not satisfactorily adjusted in three (3) working days, Step 3 should be taken.

Step 3. The grievance committee consisting of four (4) members appointed by the union shall discuss the grievance with the plant manager or his appointed representative. A representative of the International may be present at this meeting. The aggrieved employee may also be present.

Step 4. If the company and the union cannot agree on a settlement of any grievance or dispute within 72 hours after Step 3 has been taken, then the dispute between the parties may be submitted to arbitration as set forth in paragraph (b) below, providing that either party has given written notice requesting arbitration within 15 days following completion of the final meeting held under Step

3. In this event, the arbitration procedure set forth below shall prevail.

(b) The parties shall designate a mutually satisfactory arbitrator, and in the event they fail to agree upon such arbitrator within three (3) days after arbitration is requested as aforesaid, then the Federal Mediation and Conciliation Service shall, at the request of either party, furnish the company and the union with a list for the selection of an arbitrator. The list furnished by the FMCS, however, shall be restricted to the geographic area of New Jersey and metropolitan New York. The arbitrator shall hear the matter in dispute as soon as possible and render his award thereon in writing. The award of the arbitrator shall be final and conclusively binding on the parties.

(c) An attempt to settle all disputes and grievances by consultations in the manner hereinabove outlined shall be a condition precedent to arbitration and shall be of the essence of this Agreement. A demand that a matter be submitted to arbitration must in all cases take place within 35 working days after the occurrence giving rise to the dispute or grievance in question. All costs of arbitration shall be borne equally by the Company and the Union, except that each party shall procure the attendance of witnesses at its own cost and expense.

(d) Grievance within the meaning of the grievance procedure and this arbitration clause shall consist only of disputes about the interpretation or application of particular clauses of the Agreement and about alleged violations of the Agreement. The arbitrator shall have no power to add to, subtract from, or modify wage schedules or modify any of the terms of this Agreement, nor shall he substitute his discretion for that of the Company or the Union, nor shall he exercise any responsibility or function of the Company or the Union.

· (e) The Company agrees to pay those employees involved in the above grievance procedure for all time lost from their regularly scheduled shift. Payments will not be made to those employees attending grievance meetings held at times other than their regularly scheduled working hours, nor will the Company pay for the time spent in grievance meetings that may carry over beyond the end of the regularly scheduled shift.

An example of a grievance procedure which does not terminate in arbitration follows. It is contained in a contract between a Hospital Association and a State Nurses Association.

Hospital Conference Committee:
The hospital administrator and the director of nursing service, jointly with the elected representatives of general duty nurses of said Hospital, shall constitute a hospital conference committee to assist with personnel problems. Such committee shall be on a permanent basis and shall meet regularly.

In the event misunderstandings or disagreements shall arise with respect to the meaning or interpretation of this Agreement, or with respect to related questions, attempts to settle such misunderstandings or disagreements shall be normally in the following order:

A. Between persons immediately involved.

B. Between persons immediately involved and the director of nursing service.

C. Between persons immediately involved, the director of nursing service, and the administrator. At this meeting the nurse or nurses involved have the privilege of requesting the presence of the general duty conference committee members.

D. If the agreement is not reached, the hospital conference committee shall strive toward a solution of the problem.

E. If agreement is not arrived at on a local level, then a committee composed of five representatives of the

State Hospital Council and five representatives of the Union shall meet with both parties concerned for the purpose of making recommendations on any issue that may arise regarding the interpretation of this Agreement.

Federal Grievance Procedures

Labor-management relations in the federal sector are controlled primarily by Executive Order 11491, amended by Executive Order 11616 in 1971, to modify Section 13, entitled "Grievance and Arbitration Procedures." The new section reads as follows:

(a) An agreement between an agency and a labor organization shall provide a procedure, applicable only to the unit, for the consideration of grievances over the interpretation or application of the agreement. A negotiated grievance procedure may not cover any other matters, including matters for which statutory appeals procedures exist, and shall be the exclusive procedure available to the parties and the employees in the unit for resolving such grievances. However, any employee or group of employees in the unit may present such grievances to the agency and have them adjusted, without the intervention of the exclusive representative, as long as the adjustment is not inconsistent with the terms of the agreement and the exclusive representative has been given opportunity to be present at the adjustment.

(b) A negotiated procedure may provide for the arbitration of grievances over the interpretation or application of the agreement, but not over any other matters. Arbitration may be invoked only by the agency or the exclusive representative. Either party may file exceptions to an arbitrator's award with the Council, under regulations prescribed by the Council.

(c) Grievances initiated by an employee or group of employees in the unit on matters other than the interpretation or application of an existing agreement may be presented under any procedure available for the purpose.

(d) Questions that cannot be resolved by the parties as to whether or not a grievance is on a matter subject to the grievance procedure in an existing agreement, or is subject to arbitration under that agreement, may be referred to the Assistant Secretary for decision.

(e) No agreement may be established, extended or renewed after the effective date of this Order which does not conform to this section. However, this section is not applicable to agreements entered into before the effective date of this Order.

Under the amended Section 4, the Federal Labor Relations Council may consider, subject to its regulations, "exceptions to arbitration awards." A booklet entitled *The Arbitration Process*, issued by the Department of the Navy, gives the following interpretation of Section 4 as it applies to the finality of the arbitrator's award: "Thus where the parties negotiate a procedure that calls for arbitration, the arbitrator's decision must be accepted by the parties. Challenges to any award should be sustained only on grounds similar to those applied by the courts in private sector labor-management relations, and procedures for the consideration of exceptions on such grounds must be developed by the Federal Labor Relations Council." (Generally, in the private sector, an award can be modified or set aside only if it can be established that there was fraud or misconduct, or that the arbitrator clearly exceeded his authority, or that the award is contrary to law or other controlling regulations.)

Elements of an Effective Grievance Procedure

1. All grievances should be reduced to writing and signed by the grievant on a special grievance form.
2. The company's answer should be in writing.

3. Time limits should be set within which a grievance must be filed after the incident giving rise to the dispute occurs.

4. The company should be required to answer within certain time limits, e.g., 48 hours.

5. If the union is not satisfied with the company's answer it should be required to appeal to the second step within a limited period of time, e.g., five working days.

6. The company should be required to submit its second step answer within the same time limits.

7. All subsequent steps should have time limitations.

8. Time limits should be strictly adhered to. The parties will waive their rights if they do not follow the time limitations.

9. Both management and the union should encourage their representatives to settle grievances at the lower steps in the grievance procedure.

10. Adequate opportunity should be given to representatives of both management and the union to fully investigate the grievance.

11. Provision should be made for the priority handling of grievances involving discharge, suspension, or other disciplinary action.

6 | The Decision-Making Process

INTRODUCTION

Conflict occurs when individuals or groups of people viewing the same situation have different desires or come to different conclusions. In labor-management relations, conflict occurs when, for example, management decides that it will offer a 10-cent an hour wage increase and no increase in pensions while the union decides that unless it obtains a 20-cent-an-hour increase in wages and an increase in pension benefits they will strike. Or management decides that it has just cause to discharge Mr. Jones, while Mr. Jones and his union representative decide that management has no grounds. There may be conflicting decisions on the part of management and labor which generate grievances regarding such problems as equitable distribution of overtime, seniority rights, premium pay, holiday and vacation pay, and so forth. Many of these disputes are submitted to arbitrators who must analyse the decision-making process used by the parties in order to determine the points of conflict.

In order to resolve grievances it is most important for both management and labor representatives to be fully aware of the process by which each has arrived at his decision. If they are able to see clearly why they disagree, many disputes can be settled without going to arbitration. When an employee is disciplined for insubordination, the resulting grievance cannot be settled if one side repeats over and over that the employee was insubordinate and the other side says he was not. An anal-

ysis must be made of why each side came to a different conclusion. If the foreman says that the employee refused to obey
an order and the employee says he did not refuse to obey, we
have a question of fact that must be determined. What the foreman may consider a refusal may be different from what the employee considers a refusal. These differing conclusions may be
the result of different cultures, for example.

Unfortunately, most people do not know why they have
made a particular decision, which they may honestly believe
is right. They simply try to find arguments to justify what they
have already decided.

For example, marital conflict may be the result of differing
cultural patterns regarding how to bring up children, whether
a wife should work, whether the husband of a working wife
should do the shopping, cooking, or dishes. Each partner has
his or her own preconceived ideas. Their arguments merely
justify conclusions based upon differing cultural concepts.

The tendency to rationalize decisions is characteristic of
even very well-educated people. Both management and
unions retain lawyers to think up arguments to justify their decisions. It is the function of the arbitrator to evaluate these arguments.

Most people are captives of their culture, which is the result of parental and peer-group influences and certain critical
experiences. Their decisions are based upon acquired habits
of thinking which are seldom analyzed. The first step in the
resolution of conflict is to analyze the influence of basic cultural concepts on the decision-making process. This includes an
analysis of our attitudes regarding what constitutes proper employee-employer relations.

ELEMENTS OF THE DECISIONAL PROCESS

In the process of making a decision, certain elements must be
considered. By analyzing them we become aware of how they
influence our decisions, and we can thus avoid making "gut"

decisions without knowing why, and trying to justify them later.

Facts

A fact is something that is not in dispute, such as an employee's date of hire, age, position on the seniority list, and so forth.

To establish the facts it is necessary for both parties to keep accurate records that can be produced at grievance or arbitration hearings. It is good practice for labor and management to stipulate to the facts before arguing about the grievance. They may find, for instance, that they disagree because they are working from two different seniority lists. This applies to each step in the grievance procedure as well as arbitration hearings.

Allegations

An allegation is a claim made against someone. It must be distinguished from a fact.

If an employee complains to his shop steward that his foreman has not given him a fair share of overtime work, this is merely an allegation. Unless the shop steward checks the overtime records and verifies the allegation, he should not file a grievance.

A new foreman recommends to the personnel department that an employee be disciplined for insubordination, claiming he used foul language in talking to him. The claim that the employee was guilty of insubordination is merely an allegation. If an investigation discloses, for example, that it has been common practice for employees, including foremen, to use foul language to each other in the shop, it cannot be considered insubordination.

Unfortunately, shop stewards, grievance committeemen, foremen, supervisors, and other managers often treat allegations as facts without verifying them. Arbitrators will only treat allegations as facts if the records and testimony support the allegations.

Assumptions

An assumption is a concept one assumes to be true without proof. A large number of disagreements which result in grievances are based upon assumptions. Our assumptions are often based on our culture. For instance, if we see a young man with long hair and bare feet, we make certain assumptions about his character.

• A manager of industrial relations saw an employee sitting on a high ladder with his arms crossed doing no work. On the basis of this incident he assumed that the employee was irresponsible and not worthy of the promotion recommended by his foreman. A grievance was filed. At the arbitration hearing the employee explained that he had crossed his arms on the ladder because while he was moving heavy pipe from one bin to another he noticed that the manager of industrial relations and some other company executives were about to walk under his ladder, and he wanted to avoid an accident. The manager of industrial relations admitted that he and other executives had walked under the ladder, and that this incident was the only basis for his conclusion that the employee should not be promoted. The arbitrator upheld the grievant.

• A company doctor reported to the personnel manager that he was struck by an employee. The employee was immediately discharged, and filed a grievance. At the hearing the doctor was cross-examined. His testimony revealed that he had heard his secretary and the grievant in his outer office having an argument, and had rushed out of his office and grabbed the man by his jacket to throw him out. The grievant fought back.

It was obvious at the end of the hearing that the assumptions made by the personnel manager when he summarily discharged the employee were incorrect.

• A black employee claimed that his foreman always assigned him the most difficult jobs. The shop steward, assuming that this was true, filed a grievance charging discrimination. It was disclosed at the arbitration hearing that there was one difficult job in the department, but that it was rotated among all the men in the department. The grievance was denied.

Opinions

Opinions are conclusions arrived at by persons who have the technical or professional ability to evaluate a situation. In order for an opinion to be valid, the person expressing it must have expertise in the subject matter evaluated and sufficient facts on which to base his conclusion. For example, the opinion that an employee is seriously ill is only valid if expressed by a physician who has examined the employee. The opinion that Mr. Jones is not a good tool and die maker is valid only if the person expressing this opinion is an experienced, first-class tool and die maker who has observed, over a period of time, the workmanship of Mr. Jones.

• A foreman expressed to his supervisor the opinion that John Doe, who had been transferred to his department three weeks previously, was irresponsible because he had been absent three days and late four days. John Doe was given a two-day disciplinary layoff, and filed a grievance. At the arbitration hearing his timecards indicated that he had been absent only once during the previous year for illness and was never late. He testified that during the three-week period in question his wife and mother had had to be rushed to the hospital, leaving him the responsibility of getting his children off to school. Since the foreman had not known all the facts, his opinion of John Doe was not valid.

• In a wage arbitration the union insisted on a substantial wage increase. To support its position, the union argued that since all the employees had been fully employed in the past year and even had worked overtime, business must be very good. The company claimed it had lost money.

The company produced records to prove that most of the goods produced had not been sold but had been put in a warehouse in anticipation of increased demand during the spring season. Instead, there had been a sudden drop in demand throughout the entire industry and the goods had had to be sold below cost, causing a loss, not a profit. Obviously the union's opinion was invalid because it did not have all the facts.

Personality

Each human being has many characteristics which collectively determine his personality. The nature of his personality often determines his decisions. Two individuals presented with the same set of facts will often come to different conclusions because they have different personalities.

• In one case the department head, an engineer, saw an employee sitting on two upturned oil drums next to his work station with his eyes closed and head down. The employee had been assigned to watch a plastic substance ooze slowly out of a funnel. If the plastic stopped coming out of the funnel, he was to notify his foreman. The department head said nothing to the employee, but instead went to see the foreman, told him what he had seen, and said "Take care of the situation." The foreman went to the employee, shook his shoulder, and told him to get off the oil drums and pay more attention to his work. Later the department head asked his foreman whether he had taken care of the matter. The foreman said yes and told the department head what he had done. The department head became very angry with the foreman and told him to go back and discharge the employee for sleeping on the job. The employee filed a grievance claiming he was not asleep. At the arbitration hearing it became very obvious that the personalities of the department head and foreman were quite different. The department head was a domineering person who felt that employees had to "toe the line," and that any deviation warranted discharge. The foreman, with a different personality, took into consideration that the incident had occurred about 4 p.m. on a very hot summer day and that the employee involved had a good work record, and came to the conclusion that discharge was not warranted.

• In another case, an aggressive shop steward took a delight in filing grievances and arguing with the foreman. He merely assumed, without further investigation, that the employees were always right. As a result of his aggressive personality it was almost impossible to settle any grievances. The following year a nonaggressive, businesslike shop steward was elected. Thereafter the number of grievances dropped, and most were settled without arbitration. The personality of a person, which is often influenced by his cultural background, frequently makes a difference in the decisions he makes.

Weighting

Weighting refers to the importance the decision-maker gives to a fact, allegation, or opinion. For example, an employee is asked to work overtime and refuses. To some foremen this is a very serious offense which may warrant severe disciplinary action, while to others it is not. The importance people give to certain events varies considerably depending on their personalities, value judgments, and culture; therefore, weighting affects the final decision.

• In one rather amusing situation an attorney for a company was cross-examining a woman shop steward who had testified on behalf of a male shop steward who was the grievant. To prove that her testimony was biased in favor of the grievant, he asked her whether they were engaged to be married. The witness responded that although they were living together she was not engaged to and would never marry the grievant. The attorney appeared embarrassed and apologized to the witness for bringing up the subject. The witness told the attorney that there was nothing to be embarrassed about so there was no need for his apology.

In some cultures being prompt for appointments and getting to work on time is very important. In other cultures lateness is rather expected. If young people come from an environment where there is a high rate of unemployment, getting to work on time and every day is not considered important.

Our culture determines the weight we give to horseplay, vulgar language, obedience to orders, and so forth. In some cultures horseplay and the use of vulgar language are considered normal and proper behavior. In other cultures, such behavior is repulsive.

When a person makes a decision, he unconsciously gives each incident a certain weight, and will take it for granted that the weight he gives it is the only proper weight. Differences in weighting often result in different decisions. This is the reason why it is important for people who are trying to settle a grievance to analyze the weight given to each event.

Quantum of Proof

The amount of proof needed varies directly with the seriousness of the allegations. Let us assume that an employee has been discharged by the plant manager on the recommendation of his foreman, who claims he was stealing. The employee denies he stole. Under our American concept of justice a man is presumed innocent until proven guilty. If the only evidence submitted is that certain tools to fix motors have disappeared from the department and the discharged employee fixes motors in his spare time on weekends and could use these tools, the evidence is insufficient to sustain the discharge for theft. The proof would be much stronger if the tools were found in his locker, even though the employee claimed someone else put them there to frame him. But note the following case heard by the author.

• An employee in a New York department store was discharged for stealing. She filed a grievance claiming she had been framed by other employees. The testimony established that as the grievant was leaving the store her packages were inspected, as usual, by a member of the security department, who found a black dress belonging to the store. The employee immediately stated that she must have taken the black dress instead of her own dark blue dress by error because, she claimed, they had been hanging on adjacent hooks. She was brought back into the security office so that her story could be checked. While there, the chief of security noted her large bulging handbag and asked her to open it. When she did, out came two nightgowns belonging to the store. The employee immediately denied taking them and charged that she was being framed by other employees. The chief of security testified that he was much surprised to find the merchandise in her handbag because the grievant was a long-time employee with an excellent reputation. However, since she had been caught with the merchandise in her possession, he had no choice but to report the incident to top management.

Further testimony revealed that two departments had been consolidated and the grievant, who was black, was designated to head both departments because of her long years of excellent service. The supervisor of the other department, who was white, was discharged. Immediately after this event the employees who were supervised by the grievant, most of whom were white, became antagonistic toward the grievant.

It was also revealed that the nightgowns were not the grievant's size, and were made of almost transparent purple and pink materials. The grievant was a middle-aged woman who used no makeup and was a deaconess in her church. The dark blue dress owned by the grievant was found where she said she left it.

After two days of hearings, it was very clear to all who heard the testimony that the grievant was not guilty of stealing, even though the merchandise was found in her handbag.

• In another example, an employee was alleged to have used foul language to another employee, and was given a written warning by his foreman. The employee denied he had used the alleged language, and filed a grievance. At the hearing the employee against whom the alleged foul language had been used denied that it had been. However, two foremen testified that they heard the grievant use the alleged language. If the arbitrator believed that the two foremen were credible witnesses and that the other employee was merely protecting the grievant, he would probably find there was sufficient proof to support the allegation and sustain the penalty.

Appropriate Penalty—Corrective Discipline

If management finds that disciplinary action is warranted, it must then decide what is an appropriate penalty. This may range from a written reprimand to discharge.

After listening to cases for 30 years, the author has found that for the same offense the penalty decided on may range from a written reprimand to discharge, depending on the personality and cultural background of the person making the decision.

Let us assume that an employee talks back to his foreman loudly while questioning an order. One foreman, taking into consideration that he is normally a good employee with many years of service who is very upset over a family situation, might merely give him a written warning. Another foreman, feeling that an employee's family troubles should not affect his working relationships, and that an employee is obligated to follow orders without question, may decide to discharge him.

There appears to be a tendency among old-time foremen and supervisors to discharge for almost any offense. This is the reason why many arbitration awards reduce the penalty.

Arbitrators have developed two important concepts: (1) The penalty must fit the offense, and (2) the purpose of most discipline is to correct, not punish, improper behavior.

Our entire system of justice is based upon the concept that the penalty imposed must bear a direct relationship to the offense committed. An employee who is charged with lateness should not be given the same penalty as a person charged with stealing.

Yet in spite of this theory, a recent study of decisions rendered by judges in the State of New York disclosed that for exactly the same offense, different penalties were imposed depending on what part of the state the judge hearing the case was located in and the ethnic and racial characteristics of the defendant. It is also interesting to note that 400 or 500 years ago, penalties were related to the social status of the defendant. The higher the status, the lower the penalty.

The concept of corrective discipline, sometimes called progressive discipline, implies that the purpose of discipline is to correct improper behavior. If an employee has a bad absenteeism record but is otherwise a good employee, the objective of discipline is to try to correct his bad record. The first penalty imposed may be a one-day disciplinary layoff. If he continues to be absent, he may be given a one-week disciplinary layoff. If his continued absence is disrupting production schedules, discharge may be appropriate.

Under normal conditions an arbitrator will not sustain a discharge for absenteeism for the first offense. He will reduce the penalty and suggest the application of the concept of corrective discipline. Most well-managed companies follow the principle of corrective discipline.

Important Points

Factors involved in the decision-making process are:
1. Facts.
2. Allegations.
3. Assumptions.
4. Opinions.
5. Personalities.
6. Weighting.
7. Quantum of proof.
8. Appropriate penalty.
9. Corrective discipline.

Summary

When different people viewing the same situation come to different decisions, conflict occurs. This may result in a grievance or even a strike. It is, therefore, of utmost importance that management and labor each examine their decision-making process carefully before coming to a decision.

The most important step the shop steward should take is to investigate thoroughly the allegations of the employee who wishes to file a grievance. If the employee has no case, he should tell him so and give reasons. If the steward feels there is some evidence to support the grievance, he should file it even though he may have doubts because he serves as an advocate for the employee.

In the process of making a decision to file or not file a grievance, he should not rely on assumptions or opinions unless verified. Moreover, he should not permit his negative or positive feelings for the employee or supervisor to influence his decision.

The party who observes the following rules will be in a much better position to win his case:

1. Distinguish between facts and allegations and investigate every allegation thoroughly.
2. Do not make a decision based upon assumptions.
3. Check opinions for accuracy before making a decision.
4. Distinguish between serious and minor offenses.
5. Follow the concepts of corrective discipline.
6. Distinguish between long-service employees and those recently employed.
7. Be sure the penalty fits the offense.
8. Be consistent. For similar offenses involving different employees the penalties must be similar.

7 | Preparing the Case for Arbitration

THE ARBITRATION CLAUSE

If the company and the union are unable to settle a grievance they will usually proceed to arbitration. Almost all union contracts provide for arbitration as the final step in the grievance procedure. A typical clause would read as follows:

> If any dispute shall arise between the union and the employer in connection with the construction, interpretation, validity, or performance of this agreement, the union and the employer shall make an earnest endeavor to settle any such dispute between them. If they fail to reach a satisfactory adjustment, such dispute shall be submitted to arbitration; however, no dispute may be submitted to arbitration without the written consent of the other party more than sixty (60) days after the occurrence of the events giving rise to the dispute.
>
> Pending a decision of the arbitrator and thereafter so long as the employer shall abide by the arbitrators' award, the union will not cause, sanction, or take part in any strike, walkout, picketing, or stoppage of work.
>
> The arbitrator shall not have the power to add to, modify, or change any of the provisions of this agreement. The decision of such arbitrator shall be final and conclusive upon the parties hereto, who agree to abide by such decision during the term of this agreement and further agree that the decision of such arbitrator may be enforced by appropriate action by any court of competent jurisdiction.

It should be noted that this clause provides:

1. The grievance must relate to an interpretation of the collective bargaining agreement.
2. The parties must endeavor to settle the dispute.
3. The submission to arbitration must be within certain time limitations.
4. The union is prohibited from striking.
5. The arbitrator has no power to change or add to the provisions of the contract. His power is limited to an interpretation of the agreement.
6. The arbitrator's award is final and binding.
7. The award may be enforced in a court of law.

Selecting the Arbitrator

Arbitrators are selected by mutual agreement of the company and the union in one of the following three ways: (1) by direct agreement of the company and the union, (2) by selecting an acceptable arbitrator from a list submitted to the parties by an arbitration agency, or (3) by agreeing to the appointment of a permanent arbitrator.

Direct Selection by the Parties

The international representative and attorney for the union may meet with the director of industrial relations and the attorney representing the company and jointly agree on a specific person as the arbitrator. Frequently the arbitrator receives a letter signed by both the union and the company asking him to serve.

Selection Through an Agency

The American Arbitration Association is a private agency that maintains a list of qualified arbitrators. Lists of arbitrators are also maintained by the Federal Mediation and Conciliation Service in Washington, D.C., as well as by several state mediation agencies.

A list of approved arbitrators may be requested from one of these agencies. For example, upon receipt of such a request the New York State Board of Mediation sends out the following form letter:

> This Board has been asked by the Union-Employer to designate an arbitrator in the dispute stated above. The arbitrator will be designated from among the five persons (biographical sketches enclosed) selected from our panel of arbitrators whose names appear below.
>
> On the enclosed duplicate, please delete not more than two names, and indicate your preference among the remainder by numbering them 1, 2, 3. Sign the list and return immediately to this office. This same opportunity is being extended to the other party. Upon receipt of the lists from both parties the arbitrator will be designated.

Permanent Arbitrator

Where the collective bargaining contract covers a large number of employees and a great many grievances are submitted to arbitration, the parties frequently designate a person as the permanent arbitrator to whom all disputes are referred. He is sometimes called Impartial Chairman and serves for the term of the labor contract.

THE COLLECTIVE BARGAINING AGREEMENT

Contract Provisions

It is of utmost importance that the supervisor and the shop steward know in detail the terms and conditions of the labor contract. Each shop steward must know not only the rights the union has under the contract but also the limitations on these rights. For instance, an employee has the right to file a grievance, but unless he does so within a specified period of time after the grievance arises, he loses this right. Even the right to arbitration may be lost unless a demand for arbitration is made within a certain short period of time after the company gives its final answer.

A grievance is usually defined as a dispute over the interpretation of the contract. Unless the shop steward knows his contract he does not know whether he has a legitimate grievance which will be upheld by an arbitrator.

The supervisor must also know the contract. Any failure to read and know in detail the provisions of the agreement may result in losing the case. In one case a supervisor refused to give a raise to a new employee who had been on the job for six months because he thought his work was not completely satisfactory. He failed to notice that the contract provided for an automatic increase after six months. The contract gave him no choice but to give the automatic increase or discharge the employee before the end of the six-month period. As a result of not reading the contract the company lost the case in arbitration.

Important Points

1. Supervisors and shop stewards alike must thoroughly understand and comply with the rights given to and limitations imposed on both parties by the labor contract.

2. One important limitation is that time limits are set for each step in the grievance-arbitration procedure. Failure to meet any one of these deadlines could mean loss of the case.

Consistent Application of Contract Provisions

A company will have a very weak case before an arbitrator if it does not consistently apply the provisions of the contract. If the contract requires an employee to submit a doctor's certificate as proof of illness on the day before or the day after a scheduled paid holiday in order to entitle him to holiday pay, then the company must require the same thing of all employees.

If the company rules forbid smoking in the plant, the supervisor cannot strictly enforce the rule against certain employees and not against others. If a supervisor suspends a man for smoking in a forbidden area, the arbitrator may cancel the suspension if the union can prove that it has been common practice for the supervisor to look the other way when others have smoked in the same area.

It is of equal importance that all supervisors apply the same rule consistently. If the supervisor in one department will suspend a man for one week for smoking in a forbidden area, whereas another supervisor in a different department will give only a written warning for the same offense, an arbitrator may reduce the one-week suspension. Whether a company loses its case often depends upon whether supervisors have applied the provisions of the contract consistently.

The shop steward must also be consistent in this interpretation of the contract. If he interprets the contract one way for certain employees and in a different way for others, he will lose the respect of the men he represents as well as of his foreman. A shop steward should not diligently press grievances for certain employees and overlook the grievances of others.

Important Point

Provisions of the labor contract must be applied consistently by both parties.

Previous Interpretations of the Contract

Both the shop steward and the supervisor should be aware of how particular sections of the contract have been previously interpreted in similar cases by the company and the union. Past practice is an important factor in contract interpretations in the view of arbitrators. If a particular provision in dispute has been previously arbitrated, both the supervisor and the shop steward should read the award. Knowledge of such awards is important in deciding whether to go to arbitration.

It is a good policy for both the union and the company to prepare digests of all arbitration awards and put them into the hands of supervisors and shop stewards. These awards should be the subject of discussion at shop stewards' and supervisors' meetings.

Important Point

Shop stewards and supervisors should be aware of previous interpretations of the labor contract in similar cases, especially if a grievance should go to arbitration; past experience will influence the arbitrator considerably.

Documentation of the Case

It is important that each issue submitted to arbitration be supported whenever possible by documents. It is not enough for a supervisor to state at an arbitration hearing that he suspended an employee because he was always late. He must produce time records to prove his case.

When a man is discharged because he is a poor worker, it is important to produce production records. If no records are available, the arbitrator may be forced to decide between the word of the supervisor and the word of the employee, shop steward, and fellow workers.

A supervisor must keep a written record of prior offenses by an employee he has finally decided to discharge, or he may find himself at a decided disadvantage at the arbitration hearing if the employee denies that he committed the alleged prior offenses. It is therefore important for the supervisor and the personnel office to keep accurate records.

The best way to record offenses is to give to the employee a written record of his offense and the penalty imposed (such as oral or written warning), asking the employee to countersign the document, which is then filed in the employee's personnel record. It is not a good policy for a supervisor who reprimands an employee for committing an offense to report it orally to the personnel department, where some clerk makes a notation on the employee's personnel record. The accuracy of such notations will be automatically challenged at the arbitration hearing. The union will deny either the existence of the offense or the accuracy of the notation. The union will argue that there are two sides to every story, and that the notation in the personnel file only reflects the supervisor's side, which may be colored by the fact that he was excited or upset over the incident when he reported it. Moreover, since the notation is actually made by someone in the personnel department who does not have first-hand information and must rely on his interpretation of what the supervisor is trying to convey, inaccuracies are inevitable.

The employee will argue that although he felt the supervisor was wrong he had not felt the incident was important enough to file a formal grievance, but that if he had known that the incident was being recorded in his personnel file he would have done so.

Presenting the Facts

Before a shop steward or supervisor appears before an arbitrator he should ask himself "Do I know what the facts are? Do I know the names of the people, the dates and time involved? Do I know them well enough so that I will not be confused during cross-examination?"

Particularly when there are many facts to remember that may have taken place a year or more before, it may be necessary for the shop steward or supervisor to prepare himself for the arbitration hearing by writing out all the evidence he will present.

Additionally, he must be prepared to offer proof to substantiate what he alleges. If a supervisor wants to establish as a fact that Don Walters is a very poor worker, he should offer as proof records of production, scrap, rejects, quality control, time studies, and so forth.

It should be emphasized that an unsupported statement by a supervisor may not be sufficient to establish as a fact that an employee is a poor worker, is always absent or late, is insubordinate, uses offensive language, and so forth.

Opinions of Witnesses

The weight an arbitrator will give to an opinion depends upon the qualifications of the person expressing the opinion. A time-study engineer may be qualified to express an opinion regarding incentive standards, but not the shop steward or supervisor. The foreman in a tool and die shop is qualified to give an opinion regarding the quality of the work performed by a tool and die maker.

• In one case, a department head decided that each weaver should be responsible for 30 looms. The union filed a grievance because the employees felt that they should each operate only 28 looms. At the hearing, each side expressed an opinion but had no basis for it. The arbitrator rejected both opinions and ordered that time studies be made by a professional engineer whose opinion would be accepted. A witness who is asked to express an opinion must be qualified to do so.

If a person is called to be a witness in an arbitration hearing, he should be asked to testify only to those events of which he has personal knowledge. He should testify to what he saw, heard, and read in order to support a conclusion. If management wishes to prove that Bill Worth was insubordinate, the witness must be able to testify that he was present during the incident, saw the men involved, and heard the argument. If the witness can only say that Sam Held told him the day after the incident that Bill Worth struck the foreman, this is hearsay evidence, not direct evidence. Although hearsay evidence is admissible in arbitration hearings, unlike in courts of law, it is usually given little weight by the arbitrator.

Important Point

Witnesses should testify only about events of which they have personal knowledge, or in areas in which their opinions are backed up by expertise.

Criteria Used by Arbitrators in Similar Cases

Supervisors, shop stewards, and personnel directors should become familiar with the criteria commonly used by arbitrators in deciding cases. Knowledge of these criteria can be helpful at all stages in the grievance procedure as well as at the arbitration hearing.

For instance, an arbitrator will never sustain the discharge of an employee with long years of service for the first offense unless it is a very serious one, such as theft. In minor offenses arbitrators consider it more equitable if an employee is warned and suspended before being discharged. If supervisors and shop stewards know this they can act accordingly at the initial stages of the grievance.

If a case goes to arbitration, a study of awards in similar cases will enable the company and the union to make a more effective presentation. The Bureau of National Affairs and Commerce Clearing House publish selected arbitration awards, which should be available in the company's industrial relations office. Many international unions also publish cases in which they are involved. Digests and the full text of cases may also be obtained from the American Arbitration Association.

The Award

Most arbitration clauses provide for a final and binding award which is enforceable in the courts. The courts have no power to review a case on its merits. Since the parties have agreed to abide by the arbitrator's decision, the court is obliged to enforce this agreement. However, an award can be set aside by the court if the arbitrator has exceeded his authority, had a financial interest in the company, or if there were other grounds such as fraud or misconduct.

Some arbitration awards, by agreement of the parties, are only advisory, while several state statutes provide that awards, particularly those involving police and firemen, are final and binding.

A | Exhibits Illustrating Complete Grievance Procedures Ending in Arbitration

The following exhibits are included to illustrate how the complete grievance procedure, including arbitration as the final step, is applied in unionized companies. These are actual cases, but the names used are fictitious to protect the identity of the individuals involved. Company names have been changed as well.

EXHIBIT 1
PERFORMANCE RATING ALLEGED BY GRIEVANT TO BE UNFAIR

Background Information

This case involved a four-step grievance procedure in a large department store. Arbitration was available to either party as a fifth step if the matter was not satisfactorily settled in Step 4. The grievance procedure is as follows:

Step 1

The aggrieved employee, either individually or with his shop steward, at the employee's option, takes up the matter with his immediate supervisor, who shall give his answer within two (2) working days.

Step 2

If not settled satisfactorily at Step 1, the shop steward, or a union committee consisting of not more than three (3) members and the steward, if the committee requests his presence, submits the dispute to the departmental merchandise manager or such other supervisory executive as may be designated by the employer, who shall give his answer within three (3) working days.

Step 3

If not settled satisfactorily at Step 2, the union administrator, or other officer of the union, submits the dispute in writing to the manager of employee relations, who shall answer within five (5) working days.

Step 4

If not settled satisfactorily at Step 3, the union administrator or other officer of the union submits the dispute to the vice president in charge of personnel or his authorized representative, who shall answer within two (2) working days.

Arbitration (Step 5)

If the union and the employer fail to reach a satisfactory adjustment of the dispute (at Step 4) it shall be submitted to arbitration by the party desiring arbitration within sixty (60) days after the occurrence of the events giving rise to the dispute. The party desiring arbitration shall notify the other in writing of its intention to arbitrate the dispute.

The grievant, Ed Evans, has been an employee of the store for 33 years, for the last 19 in a department where large, expensive appliances are sold. He had been one of the top salesmen in the department and one of the highest paid in the store.

The company gives annual performance ratings to all employees with more than one year of service. Each employee is rated on 11 factors, and the ratings range from "excellent" to "unsatisfactory." The purpose of the performance reviews is to determine the caliber of the work force, identify strong performance, reward employees for such performance, and identify substandard performance, in order to encourage improvement or to determine the need for termination of employment. One way in which salesmen are rewarded for outstanding performance is that those who are rated excellent in three factors— "manner and interest in customers," "alertness to service," and "cooperation"—are placed on the top "eligibility list" for promotion to higher paying positions. Unless a salesman receives excellent on all three of these factors, he is put on the second-highest eligibility list.

Ed Evans had been rated excellent in these three factors for several years, and therefore had been on the preferred list. At the most recent annual review, however, he was rated only "good" on all three of the factors mentioned above, and was placed on the second-highest list instead of the top list for promotion. He filed a grievance claiming that he had been rated unfairly. The grievance was processed through all steps of the procedure, including arbitration.

Steps in Ed Evans' Grievance Procedure

Direct quotations from the grievance presentation and the company's answers have been used where possible without revealing the identity of the people, company, or union involved in the dispute.

Step 1

Mr. Evans' written grievance was as follows:

> "I have just been given a job review, as a result of which I am now on the second-highest eligibility list as against the top list. I now want clear and accurate answers with supporting information to the following questions:
>
> "(1) Why was this job review given five months after its effective date and on the day before my vacation?

"(2) Why change my rating for 'manner and interest' from excellent to good? It was admitted that I am excellent in this category, but only to those whom I think will buy, and that the reviewer did not know of any mistakes in judgment I had made.

"(3) Why change 'alertness to service' from excellent to good? Since I was told by the reviewer that I was too 'selective' in both this and the previous category, I think that (a) one or the other should be eliminated, or (b) perhaps they should be combined, or (c) both reviewer and employees should be made aware of whatever difference there may be.

"(4) Why change 'cooperation' from excellent to good? Since I was told that my cooperation with the other eight people in the department was excellent, I should like to know exactly what incidents took place and who was involved, resulting in this change.

"It also seems that there is a clear, consistent pattern of downgrading everyone in the department from their previous ratings, and that job reviews will be given just prior to going on vacation. It is my distinct impression that the present reviewers not only are ignorant of previous reviews but also feel that they do the job much better than the previous reviewers. If they can't come up with some better reasons for the changes than those I have heard, then I think they are doing a remarkably poor job."

Mr. Evans' immediate supervisor replied in writing to these four points as follows:

"(1) The annual job review period was from March 1, 19__ to March 1, 19__. The job review conference with the department sales manager, the assistant department sales manager, a personnel department representative, and myself was held on March 29th and released for interview the week of April 12th. Interviews were started immediately.

"(2) Mr. Evans told me that he thought the company was only interested in volume, to which I answered that it was interested in all customers, whether they bought or were only seeking information for future purchases in the department. To be rated excellent in 'manner and interest in customer,' a clerk must show a 'most pleasing and interested manner to all.' Mr. Evans had been rated correctly as good since he shows sincere interest in the needs of those customers he determines are going to buy. The store does not instruct him to be selective but to be 'most pleasing to all.' I did not say I had not observed any mistakes in judgment, nor that I had not had any customer complaints on his manner and interest.

"(3) In our 1 ½ hour conference, if the difference between 'manner and interest' and 'alertness to service' was not clear, Mr. Evans should have asked for a clarification, since I was prepared to spend as much time as was needed. To be rated excellent, Mr. Evans should 'immediately approach waiting customers and acknowledge waiting customers.' He was rated good, since he is 'quick to approach waiting customers' but has to be called to help customers in the department while standing and conversing with other clerks.

"(4) Mr. Evans was rated good in 'cooperation' since he 'willingly does what he is told to do, does fair share of work, and gets along well with others.' To be rated excellent he would have to 'go out of his way to be congenial and helpful and get along unusually well.' He was told he could be more receptive to direction and criticism given him.

"In response to Mr. Evans' final comment, not all department sales people were downgraded from previous ratings, nor were any rated excellent merely because they had been so rated on previous reviews. The review covered the period already stated as it was supposed to do, with no particular relationship to vacation time. It was not the intention of the reviewers to dispute previous reviewers."

Step 2

No additional facts were presented by either party at the meeting in this step. Both parties maintained their positions.

The department sales manager's written reply was as follows: "I concur with [Mr. Evans' immediate supervisor's] comments regarding this grievance."

Step 3

The union business agent's opinions, as expressed to the manager of employee relations, may be summarized as follows:

(1) He was surprised that the department sales manager agreed completely with Mr. Evans' immediate supervisor.

(2) There *has* been a complete change in the method of reviewing employees' performance. Supervisors are taking a harder look at people; to be rated excellent, an employee must now be "super-outstanding."

(3) Clerks *have* to be selective.

(4) During Mr. Evans' recent illness, he may have relaxed a bit and not pushed himself as much as before.

(5) Customer complaints can be made that have no bearing on the clerks.

(6) These people have 25 years of service. They are professionals and the store can rely on them.

(7) There is a definite pattern in the department of downgrading the salespeople.

(8) There must be an ulterior motive for this downgrading; the supervisor may be getting even because he feels the clerks are not helping him above and beyond their job classifications.

(9) Clerks do cooperate among themselves and with the executives, however. They bend over backwards to

cooperate with their immediate supervisor, who isn't even capable.

(10) It is necessary for clerks to converse with each other on the floor.

(11) Communications between the executives and the clerks are poor.

(12) It seems impossible that the clerks have suddenly changed after all these years.

(13) How can the company completely change these ratings?

The manager of employee relations had obtained some additional information from Evans' immediate supervisor and the department sales manager. His reply to the business agent may be summarized as follows:

(1) Clerks must *not* be selective. They have been told time and time again recently that they must approach and give information to all customers. The supervisor held many meetings, usually once a month during this annual review period regarding giving service to all customers. Nothing seemed to have any impact, however, until this job review.

(2) Mr. Evans' performance was much the same before and after his operation.

(3) There has been an increase in customer complaints in the department.

(4) The primary problem is being selective in picking customers to attend to. If Evans thinks a customer wants to buy, he does an excellent job. The problem is that he ignores customers when he thinks they aren't going to buy or aren't going to buy something profitable. As an example, a customer wanted Evans to demonstrate a television set. He refused to move it so it could be demonstrated. The supervisor had to apologize to the customer and get another clerk to demonstrate it. Evans said he thought the customer wasn't going to buy anyway.

(5) Evans avoids trying to sell those appliances which do not include a sales bonus to the salesman. His attitude is that the company should pay a bonus on any appliance if they want it to be sold.

(6) Evans gives the supervisor an argument if he is criticized or directed to do something. His reaction at departmental meetings is not good. None of the sales clerks are above criticism when they fail to follow the proper sales instructions.

Step 4

This step involved a meeting between an officer of the union and the vice president in charge of personnel for the store. The meeting resulted in no additional pertinent information about the case, except that the vice president brought out the following points to illustrate Evans' lack of cooperation:

(1) Evans does not cooperate with the women in the Adjustment Office. For example, if they ask him to look up a certain sale they are having difficulty getting the facts about (salesmen keep a tissue copy of all sales checks they write), Evans frequently responds that it is their job to find out about sales, not his.

(2) Since Evans' operation a year ago, the supervisor has not expected him to do any of the heavier work involved in keeping the stock on the floor in good condition. For example, he has not been expected to lift portable television sets to return them to their proper places. But he has not cooperated by dusting off the appliances at the start of the day, or by removing extraneous material from the sales area. Also he sometimes fails to inform the supervisor that a sample ticket has been removed from an appliance (usually by a customer) so the supervisor can have a new ticket attached to the appliance. He should take the initiative in keeping the supervisor informed about such discrepancies, but doesn't. He has to be told by the supervisor to check on these details.

(3) The supervisor and the department sales manager were lenient in their performance ratings last year (their first year in charge of the department) since they felt they had not been in charge long enough to impose strict rating standards at that time.

Arbitration (Step 5)

The arbitrator's award and opinion are given verbatim below:

In the Matter of the Arbitration Between R. P. Rowe Corporation -and- Local 100-R.C.V.-AFL-CIO	Award of Arbitrator

THE UNDERSIGNED ARBITRATOR, having been designated in accordance with the Arbitration Agreement entered into by the above-named parties and having been duly sworn and having duly heard the proofs and allegations of the parties, AWARDS as follows:

1. The dispute between the company and the union involving the employee, Ed Evans, is arbitrable.

2. The grievance of Ed Evans is hereby denied.

John Doe
ARBITRATOR

Date: November 7, 19____

State of

County of

ss.

On this 7th day of November, 19__, before me personally came and appeared John Doe, to me known and known to me to be the individual described in and who executed the fore-going instrument, and he acknowledged to me that he executed the same.

In the Matter of the Arbitration Between R. P. Rowe Corporation -and- Local 100 RCV, AFL-CIO	OPINION Case No. 1330-0554-66

This arbitration, which was initiated by Local 100 RCV, AFL-CIO (hereinafter referred to as the "union"), is the result of a dispute between the union and R. P. Rowe Corporation (hereinafter referred to as the "company") over certain performance ratings given by the company to Edward Evans. The company contends that this matter is not arbitrable and that, even if it were, the performance ratings in question are reasonable and the arbitrator should not direct the company to change them. A hearing was held on September 29, 19__, at which time each side was given ample opportunity to present evidence and to cross-examine each other's witnesses. O'Day and Cohen by Michael Smith, Esq., of counsel, appeared for the union and the company was represented by H. Blank, Esq.

Facts

The company gives performance ratings annually to all employees who have worked for the company for over one year. Each employee is rated on eleven factors and the ratings run from "excellent" to "unsatisfactory." The purpose of this annual review of employees is to determine the caliber of the work force, identify strong performance and award employees for such performances, and identify substandard performances in order to encourage improvement or to determine the need for separation.

Each employee subject to this annual review is rated by three superiors: the department group manager, the department sales manager, and the department associate sales manager. Each of these three executives independently fills out rating sheets which are sent to the personnel department. At that time a member of the personnel department is assigned to discuss the rating sheets in a conference with the three executives. The personnel department member guiding the conference does not have the authority to change any of the ratings, but does try, through a discussion of the facts and circumstances upon which the ratings are based, to get the responsible executives to make their ratings as accurate as possible. Once the ratings have been finally decided upon by the three executives, the employee is informed of his ratings for the year in question.

The grievant, Ed Evans, has been an employee of the company for 33 years. Since 1946 he has been employed as a salesman in the appliance department. Mr. Evans was rated for the year from March 1, 19__, through February 28, 19__, and received a rating of "good" in the following factors: manner and interest in customers, alertness to service, and cooperation.

The highest rating an employee can obtain for any factor for which he is rated is "excellent." "Good" is the next highest rating. Aside from personal pride, the reason it is important for an employee to secure a rating of excellent in the three factors described above is that an employee must maintain an excellent rating in these factors in order to be on the "top eligibility list." This is a list from which persons seeking promotions to higher paying positions must be selected, and the "top" list must be exhausted before employees on the second highest list can be promoted.

Discussion

There are two issues involved in this case: whether the dispute in question is arbitrable and, if so, whether the company violated the collective bargaining agreement by giving Mr. Evans the three ratings of "good" instead of "excellent."

Section 7.16 of the collective bargaining agreement between the parties reads in part as follows:

> Promotions from one job classification to another . . . shall be made on the basis of seniority from among those employees eligible for such promotion where in the opinion of the Employer the ability of the employees eligible for such promotion is equal. . . . The action of the Employer shall not be subject to arbitration.

This section states that promotions "shall be made on the basis of seniority from among those employees eligible for such promotion." As previously discussed, an employee has the best opportunity of being promoted if he is on the top list. If not on this list, his chances of promotion are considerably less. It is obviously important that he be rated on a reasonable basis, not in any arbitrary or capricious manner. If the company had the right to arbitrarily put employees on or take them off the top list by giving them arbitrary ratings, Section 7.16 would become a farce. It would mean that by giving arbitrary ratings the company could in any given instance cause an employee to be put on or taken off an eligibility list, and since Section 7.16 provides that the "action of the Employer shall not be subject to arbitration," it would further mean that the company could promote employees on an arbitrary basis without question.

I feel certain this is not what the Section intends. Implicit in the language of Section 7.16 is the understanding that employees must be made eligible for promotion on a reasonable basis. It would be rather absurd to conclude that the union agreed the company could promote employees on any basis whatsoever regardless of how capricious or arbitrary.

I do not believe the fact that Section 7.16 states that the "action of the Employer shall not be subject to arbitration" alters that conclusion. I think that implicit in this exclusion is the assumption that the company has acted reasonably, not arbitrarily or capriciously.

In light of the foregoing, it is my opinion that annual performance ratings given to an employee may be reviewed by an arbitrator to determine whether such ratings were made on an arbitrary or capricious basis. Accordingly, I find the instant dispute to be arbitrable.

The next question is whether the company violated the collective bargaining agreement by giving Mr. Evans the three ratings of "good" instead of "excellent" for the year March 1, 19__, through February 28, 19__. As the contract prohibits arbitrary or capricious ratings, but does not prohibit any ratings decided on a reasonable basis, the determination of the foregoing issue depends on whether the ratings in question were reasonable, or whether they were arbitrary and capricious.

The difference between a rating of "excellent" and one of "good" in the three categories in question is very slight. A rating of excellent for the factor of "manner and interest in customer" requires an employee to have a "most pleasing and interested manner to all." A rating of "good" for the same factor requires an employee to show "sincere interest in customer's needs." The distinction between "excellent" and "good" for the category of "alertness to service" is equally slight. To receive an "excellent" rating an employee must immediately approach waiting customers and acknowledge other waiting customers. For a rating of "good" he must be "quick" to approach waiting customers. Also, there is very little difference between an "excellent" and a "good" rating for the factor of "cooperation." To obtain an excellent rating, an employee must go out of his way to be congenial and helpful and must get along unusually well with others. To secure a rating of "good" he must willingly do what he is told to do, do a fair share of work, and get along well with others.

The company presented evidence to show that it had a reasonable basis for rating Mr. Evans as "good" instead of "excellent" in the three categories in question. The arbitrator cannot probe beyond reasonableness. He cannot substitute his judgment for that of the company as long as he is satisfied that the company made a reasonable decision. Whether the arbitrator would rate Mr. Evans as "excellent" instead of "good" is of no consequence. The only thing the company must show is that it had a reasonable basis for giving the ratings it did. As this burden has been sustained by the company, the grievance is denied.

Dated: November 7, 19___

John Doe
ARBITRATOR

EXHIBIT 2

VIOLATION OF "NO-SMOKING" RULE, AND USE OF OBSCENE AND ABUSIVE LANGUAGE AGAINST SECURITY GUARD

Background Information

An employee of a large hospital, William Jones, was observed by a security guard smoking in a no-smoking area of the hospital while on his way to the exit. The guard asked him to refrain from smoking. Mr. Jones ignored the guard's request and continued walking toward the exit. When the guard confronted him, he responded with a contemptuous and very obscene remark against the guard, continued on his way, and left the hospital.

The guard repeated this incident to the security chief who, in turn, reported it to the employee's supervisor. Jones was suspended without pay for one day for smoking in a restricted area, and for his obscene and abusive remarks to the guard. The union filed a grievance which was finally arbitrated.

Steps in the Grievance Procedure

Step 1

The grievant, Jones, claimed that he was outside the hospital exit when he was accused of smoking by the guard. He also denied using obscene and abusive language against the guard.

The guard steadfastly maintained that he had challenged Jones in a no-smoking area of the hospital, and that Jones had responded with a very vile, obscene remark against him. The supervisor disagreed with Jones and his steward, and decided his suspension was justified.

Step 2

This step involved discussion between the aggrieved, his steward, and the employee relations manager. No additional facts were brought out at this meeting, except that Jones had been a satisfactory employee during his period of employment. The Employee Relations Manager's decision was that the one-day suspension was justified, primarily because of the extremely contemptuous and obscene remarks against the guard who was only doing his duty by trying to enforce the no-smoking rule. The union processed the grievance to Step 3.

Step 3

This step involved discussion between the chief steward and the Personnel Director. No additional facts were presented at this meeting. Witnesses to the alleged rule infraction and name-calling were not available. The Personnel Director believed that the guard who was respected and was not the tough type had stated the truth. The chief steward believed the grievant's statement that he was outside the hospital when the guard accosted him for smoking, and did not believe Jones had referred to the guard by a vile name. It was one man's word against another's. The Personnel Director decided that the one-day suspension was justified. The union disagreed and took the case to arbitration.

Step 4 (Arbitration)

The arbitrator's award and opinion are given verbatim below:

Award

1. There was just and proper cause under the collective bargaining agreement of the parties for the imposition of the one-day disciplinary suspension upon the griev-

ant Jones; the action of the hospital in so doing, accordingly, should be and hereby is sustained and affirmed.

2. In the setting and under the particular facts and circumstances, said discipline was amply corrective, per se, without any need or valid purpose for its inclusion or retention in the personnel record of an employee with a work history that has been uniformly excellent.

Dated: October 11, 19__   Richard Rowe
                                                          ARBITRATOR

Opinion

The very nature, type, and character of the operation of a hospital, its requirements, aims, and purposes necessitate the promulgation and enforcement of rules, regulations, and/or policy requirements of conduct or procedure such as are in essence manifest from the proscribed "Principal Offenses Against Hospital Discipline" set forth in Appendix C of the collective bargaining agreement of the parties.

Just as employees are entitled to retain their jobs on the basis of good behavior, efficiency, and honesty, so is the hospital justly entitled to a disciplined and cooperative working force and the right to discipline employees who fail to meet those standards (of good behavior, efficiency, and honesty) or who commit any one or more of the offense delineated in Appendix C.

To properly enforce and prevent the breach of its rules, regulations, and/or policy requirements of conduct and procedure by all who enter its portals (including doctors, visitors, and sundry others as well as bargaining unit employees), the hospital employs uniformed guards to patrol and police the hospital premises. The function of the uniformed guard is a most important one. Morale, discipline, and efficiency in the work force as well as the proper conduct of the operation of the hospital, in no small degree, are dependent upon the tact, understanding, and capacity of the guard to perform the duties and obligations of his job with due regard to the rights and dignity as an individual of any and all persons properly within or about the hospital premises.

The job of a uniformed guard is neither enviable nor a sinecure. The guard is charged with responsively and responsibly performing the duties and obligations of this job and is answerable to the hospital for his effective conduct thereof. No matter how tactfully, indeed how diplomatically, or with what excellence of consideration and regard for the rights and dignity of others which he may exhibit, a guard is no likely candidate for a popularity award.

The guard, nonetheless, is as justly entitled to respect for his job and regard for his individual right and dignity as is any other hospital employee. Implicit in the good behavior obligation and requirement of the employment relationship is that it be accorded to him by bargaining unit employees. What is equally essential is that the hospital see that it is so accorded, or suffer the loss of the type of guard (as here involved) who is a credit to it. Indeed, any inability of the hospital to retain guards of high caliber with an appreciative regard for the rights of people as individuals would be calculated to be equally disastrous to all employees.

It is of no critical moment as to the propriety of the one-day suspension whether the grievant was actually smoking in an unauthorized area or whether the guard in good faith honestly believed that the grievant was so engaged. What is decisive is that the proof persuasively establishes that when the guard, as required, sought to prevent an infraction which he had reasonable cause to believe was occurring by his "please don't smoke" request, he was callously and contemptuously abused by a vile epithet.

The abrasiveness of the relationship between student and school monitor is with some frequency carried over into adult life—especially with some who are still very young and spirited. It is patent from the proof that the abrasiveness here was with respect to the job per se, not the guard personally or because of any animosity toward him as an individual.

It was equally manifest that grievant is essentially a decent if erring young man with a work history that has been excellent and who was rather chagrined over the entire incident as well as his former attitude with respect to the job of a guard. When feasible and adequate, the primary purpose of discipline is corrective. It would convincingly appear that it has indeed been achieved in this case.

Dated: October 11, 19___   Richard Rowe
                                                          ARBITRATOR

B | Cases for Analysis and Discussion

The author has found that one of the most effective techniques for teaching people how to make the decisions necessary to submit a matter in dispute to arbitration as well as how to evaluate its chances for success is to encourage the decision maker to analyse cases as an arbitrator would.

Most advocates, whether representatives of labor or management, will only consider the facts and arguments which they feel support their position. They seldom consider the facts or the value of the arguments being advanced by the other side. The arbitrator must evaluate all the evidence.

• To illustrate, a company discharged a union official for excessive absenteeism and lateness. The evidence against the employee fully supported the company's charges; however, the union produced in evidence as defense hundreds of personnel files with equally bad absentee and lateness records where the employees involved were not penalized, and charged discrimination. The company lost its case, not because it did not have good evidence, but because it failed properly to evaluate the evidence produced by the union.

Set forth below are two cases, presented in order to give the reader an opportunity to test his ability to analyze data and to make an equitable decision. It should be emphasized that the arguments on both sides should be evaluated in writing. This is exactly what the arbitrator has to do, and the reader's ability to win cases will depend upon his ability to use the same criteria the arbitrator does in writing his opinion.

In Case 1, only the bare facts are presented. The reader should list the arguments that could be advanced by the company and by the union to justify their respective positions, then prepare a written opinion and award giving his or her reasons for the decision rendered.

CASE 1

Tom Jones worked for an oil refinery. One day an FBI agent appeared at the refinery and asked to interview Mr. Jones and inspect his locker. In his locker the agent found a pair of army trousers. The agent told Mr. Jones that army clothing had been stolen from an army camp located about 30 miles from the refinery. Mr. Jones denied stealing any clothing from the army camp. He claimed he purchased the pair of trousers from a friend. The FBI agent left the plant with Tom Jones. The manager of the refinery, at the end of five days, called the central office and told his superior what had occurred and that he had not seen or heard from Mr. Jones since he was taken away by the FBI. The manager was told that he should discharge Mr. Jones. A week after he left the refinery, Mr. Jones appeared, ready for work, explaining that he had been taken to Washington, D.C., for interrogation, had been indicted by a grand jury, and was awaiting trial. Upon being told he had been discharged, Mr. Jones filed a grievance claiming he had been improperly discharged.

Case 2 has been set up as an actual arbitration case, giving the positions of the company and of the union, but the arbitrator's opinion and award have been separated from the rest of the case so that the reader can have the opportunity to write out his own opinion and award first, before going on to read the opinion of the arbitrator.

CASE 2

In the Matter of the Arbitration Between

United Ironworkers of America,

Local Union 0000

-and-

Federal Pipe Company

. . .

Issue

Did the company unjustly discharge Mr. T?

Position of the Company

The company alleges that Mr. T. was properly discharged for violating a company rule.

The company explained that while under indictment Mr. T. was continued as an employee, but was discharged when he pleaded guilty to a morals charge. [The exact nature of his offense was not disclosed during arbitration, but it was not rape.—Ed.]

The company claims that its policy with respect to employees under indictment for crime is that the employee is innocent until proven guilty, but that when found guilty, the employee is immediately discharged. This rule of conduct, according to the company, has been in effect for years and has been administered uniformly.

Mr. T. has been employed by the company in the shipping department for 17 years and had knowledge of the rule that employees are terminated when found guilty of crimes.

In reply to a request by the son of the grievant that he be given a leave of absence, the company states that its policy did not allow leaves of absence.

The company points out that Mr. T. had been sentenced to two to three years in prison. About one month later this sentence was modified and he was placed on probation for three years and ordered to obtain psychotherapy.

The company argues that "The modification of the sentence handed down by the court did not change his guilt. . . . The crime committed by Mr. T., of moral turpitude, was a crime against society, and his guilt and conduct do not deserve consideration for employment in our organization."

The company concludes that Mr. T. was properly discharged.

Position of the Union

The union alleges that the discharge of Mr. T. was not justified for several reasons. Under Article XVIII of the collective bargaining contract, the company is empowered "to make reasonable rules." It is argued by the union that the rule under which Mr. T. was discharged is not reasonable. It is not reasonable, according to the union, to place a man in double jeopardy. Mr. T. has already been punished by the courts for his offense against society and it is not proper for the company to punish him again by discharging him.

This rule is also unreasonable because discharge under it is the direct result of a conviction per se and is in no way related to any detriment to the company.

The union argues that if Mr. T. were reemployed, the company would suffer no harm or inconvenience, as he is employed in the shipping department and the nature of his work is unrelated to the crime he committed.

Moreover, when a company makes a rule it is obligated to reduce it to writing and make sure that both the union and employees are notified of the rule before it is enforced.

It is alleged by the union that neither the union nor the grievant was aware of the rule under which he was discharged.

Mr. T., the Union points out, must continue to make a living in our society, and there is no reason why he should not continue to work for the company where he has worked satisfactorily for 17 years.

The union concludes that the discharge of Mr. T. was not justified.

[NOTE: The opinion of the arbitrator in Mr. T.'s case follows. The serious reader should take time at this point to write out his or her own opinion before going on to read the arbitrator's. It should be emphasized that unless the reader writes out his own opinion *before* reading the actual opinion and award, he will have lost the value of this exercise in decision making. Experience has shown that the reader is usually surprised when he compares his method of analysis to that of the arbitrator.]

CASE 2
Opinion of the Arbitrator

The issue before us is whether Mr. T. was unjustly discharged. He was discharged under an alleged company rule which provides that when an employee is convicted of a "crime" he is immediately discharged. It is further alleged that this rule was used by the company on two previous occasions when employees had been convicted of "crimes." One employee was convicted of arson and the other of disposing of a body after death.

The union argues that the rule was admittedly never reduced to writing, nor was it communicated to the officials of the union or to the employees. The union argues that no employee can be disciplined for an act unless the company's rule covering such an act has been communicated to the employee.

It is a well-accepted principle of industrial relations that management has the right to discipline employees for certain acts such as fighting, insubordination, stealing, intoxication, etc. The penalties imposed, however, must be for just cause and reasonable. It is not necessary for a company to publish a list of rules of conduct listing offenses and the penalties to be imposed for each offense before an employee can be disciplined.

For instance, it is not necessary for a company to prove that all employees were notified of a written rule specifying that discharge is the penalty for theft in order to justify a discharge for theft. However, when a company seeks to impose a penalty which is somewhat unusual or severe, then it must put employees on notice before they can justify the imposition of such a penalty.

For instance, let us assume that a company wishing to correct a lateness problem made a rule that anyone who was two minutes late would be docked three hours pay. Assuming that the company could justify such a rule, they would be obligated to prove that the employee affected had been notified of the rule.

There are, therefore, two categories of rules. Those rules which cover the usual offenses, and provide the usual penalties, do not have to be communicated before the penalty is imposed. Rules, however, which provide unusual penalties should be communicated before the penalty stated in the rule is automatically imposed. In sum, although it is advisable for a company to give to each employee a written copy of all company rules, the failure to do so does not prevent the company from imposing reasonable penalties for common offenses.

The alleged rule under which Mr. T. was discharged provides for automatic discharge upon conviction of a "crime." The term crime is not defined. Presumably an employee could be discharged under this rule for the commission of any crime. In some states it is a crime to disseminate birth control information. Would conviction of an employee for this crime justify automatic discharge? A violation of certain motor vehicle laws might constitute a crime. Would such a crime justify automatic discharge?

Obviously such a generalized rule might result in some unusual and unreasonable penalties. Before an employee can be automatically penalized under the alleged rule, the term crime should be clearly defined and each employee should be notified of the existence of the rule.

There is no evidence that the alleged rule was reduced to writing. The preponderance of the evidence supports the contention of the union that neither the union officials nor the employees had knowledge of the rule.

Under these conditions the company cannot justify the automatic discharge of Mr. T. under the alleged rule.

The next question is whether the company had just cause to discharge Mr. T. under its general power to discipline.

Mr. T. did commit a wrong act against society, and the court, representing society, imposed a penalty. The wrong was primarily against society, not against the company. It did not involve company employees. It was not committed on company property nor on company time. There is no evidence that it hurt the company's business. Nor is the nature of the wrong related to the nature of the work performed by Mr. T. If Mr. T. were a route salesman, the potential harm to the company's business would be obvious. Mr. T. works in the shipping department of a foundry, however, and it is highly improbable that his continued employment in this department would be harmful to the company.

Moreover, there is no evidence that his fellow employees would be harmed, nor is there evidence that they object to his presence in the shipping department.

It is most significant in this case that Mr. T. was released from jail after 28 days and placed on probation and required to undergo psychotherapy. This is a clear indication that the court felt that he was not a danger to society and that this was essentially a medical problem.

Because of the seriousness of the issue before us, a study was made of similar cases that have been reported. It appears to be the consensus among arbitrators that being found guilty of a crime is not just cause for discharge where the crime was not committed on company property or on company time, does not involve company personnel, does not adversely affect company business, and is not related to work performance.

I therefore find that Mr. T. was unjustly discharged. He shall be reinstated without back pay.

John Doe
ARBITRATOR

Index